MW00960269

Even If Not

Even If Not: Living, Loving, and Learning in the in Between

© 2016 Kaitlyn Bouchillon

All rights reserved. No part of this publication may be reproduced, stored in a retrieval system, or transmitted in any form or by any means—for example, electronic, photocopy, recording—except for brief quotations in printed reviews, without the prior permission of the author. For inquires and permission requests, contact through the author's website: www.kaitlynbouchillon.com.

Designed by Kaitlyn Bouchillon
Edited by Alexandra Ruark

All interior photos © Kaitlyn Bouchillon. They are available as printable downloads at www.kaitlynbouchillon.com. All rights reserved.

All Scripture quotations, unless otherwise indicated, are taken from the Holy Bible, New International Version,® NIV.® Copyright © 1973, 1978, 1984, 2011 by Biblica, Inc.® Used by permission. All rights reserved worldwide.

Scripture quotations marked The Message are taken from The Message by Eugene H. Peterson, copyright © 1993, 1994, 1995, 1996, 2000, 2001, 2002. Used by permission. All rights reserved worldwide.

First printing February 2016 / Printed in the United States of America

ISBN: 1522729429

ISBN-13: 978-1522729426

"This is a book about fighting for faith & community, a book about hurting & healing, a book about living our stories & then sharing them with others. This is a book that reminds us that life in all its broken, beautiful glory is never static – it's always growing around us and connecting our highs and our lows with that ampersand – the space where most of us live. And Kaitlyn generously and bravely unpacks her in between moments to help us recognize and celebrate our own."

Lisa-Jo Baker, author of *Surprised by Motherhood* and community manager for (in)courage

"*Even If Not* is a sweet, grace-filled read to help you fill in the blanks that fall after life's question marks."

Kayla Aimee, author of *Anchored*

"Let me tell you, knowing Kaitlyn is special. Now you get to know her too. Yet, the best part about this book is not that you get to know Kaitlyn and her story, but that you get to know God and His story. Kaitlyn walks you through a path that she has walked — the beautiful and miraculous hilltops and the deepest valleys. Admitting her brokenness and utter dependency on our Savior, she imparts the wisdom she has gained from her experiences on her reader in a captivating, sweet, and impactful way. I've heard these stories before, but I found myself laughing, crying (more like weeping), and captivated all the same. I dare any reader who wants to be challenged and encouraged to pick up this book. It is the perfect combination of the two."

Kendall McPheeters, friend

"We know how to put our faith in God when He comes through for us. That's easy. But will we say that God is still good, even when life falls apart? Along comes Kaitlyn Bouchillon, a spiritual sojourner with a fresh and engaging voice, to help us. Kaitlyn tenderly leads us toward an enduring love in a trustworthy God. *Even if Not* is rich with the Gospel, sound truths, and personal stories that will inspire you. Read this book, and be challenged — in all the best ways — to let God write the story you're living."

Jennifer Dukes Lee, author of *Love Idol*

"In *Even If Not*, Kaitlyn boldly explores the paradoxes that come with following Jesus into the unknown circumstances of our daily lives. By humbly sharing her own story, full of struggles and triumphs, she challenges her readers to love, trust, and follow Jesus, especially when His plans do not match up with our own personal agenda. Through years of friendship, I've watched amazed and thankful for how Kaitlyn lives out *Even If Not* in her own life, and I cannot think of anyone else's story I would rather have a part of my library."

Alexandra Ruark, friend

"I had barely read a few pages of *Even If Not* and I was in need of a highlighter to mark profound statements I had read. Throughout the book Kaitlyn shares nuggets of truth that the reader will want to revisit — hence the need for highlighting. King David once wrote that those who love God's Word have more wisdom than the ancient and Kaitlyn's writing in *Even If Not* displays this very principle. Get out your highlighter and start mining the many nuggets that Kaitlyn has put in print."

Jackie Kendall, bestselling author
of *Lady in Waiting*

"*Even If Not* is an absolute must read! Through it, Kaitlyn offers to be that friend to talk about the ups, downs, and in betweens of life. Her open and honest style of writing encourages readers to be open and honest with themselves. She isn't afraid to speak about the not so great parts of life, but she always uses God's truth to leave readers feeling encouraged by the greatness of our loving Father."

Emerald Orbeta, friend

"*Even If Not* is a tender, gracious read that will not only help you more fully receive the love and care of your tender, gracious Savior, it will help you settle into your own spectacular life story. With wisdom beyond her years, Kaitlyn's words moved Gospel truth from my head to my heart."

Kristen Strong, author of *Girl Meets Change*

"We live in a world where the story doesn't always unfold the way we expected. In those moments we need to know we're going to be okay. We need to know we can trust the Author. We need to know whatever happens we are not done yet. That is what Kaitlyn Bouchillon beautifully, honestly, and powerfully offers our hearts in this book. When I got to the final page it didn't feel like the end; it felt like a new chapter of hope in my life was ready to begin."

Holley Gerth, *Wall Street Journal* bestselling author of *You're Already Amazing*

"In *Even If Not*, Kaitlyn passionately lures us back to the present moment, wooing us toward a life fully lived as we learn to immerse our hearts into the right-now, in between moments of life. (The good and the bad.) Wrapped tenderly in God's bountiful grace, Kaitlyn's story serves as a steadfast reminder of how He intends to use every part of our lives—no matter how broken. Her words are a permission to step away from our overbooked calendars, to surrender our best laid plans, and in the smack middle of creating a life around all those social media moments, to turn our hearts toward the certainty of a God who loves and redeems and transforms. Kaitlyn reminds us to savor His very presence. Even when life doesn't make sense."

Jo Ann Fore, bestselling author of *When A Woman Finds Her Voice*

"*Even If Not* is an invitation to trust God through the unknown and the in between. God shines so brightly through Kaitlyn's story and her faith amidst struggle. You need this book!"

Taylor Gillilan, friend

for those who are walking through an in between season . . . and for the ones who have walked with me through mine

contents

a note from the author

Here is my promise to you: every word printed in ink upon these pages is true to the very best of my memory and ability. Here is my second promise to you: it will be honest and truthful, a book full of words that are raw and real, written by a girl who has fallen for the Hero of the story.

These pages aren't full of theories or doctrine. Instead, they hold stories. God has used stories to woo me and chase me, pursuing me with words and characters and storylines too crazy and beautiful to be true, and yet they are. Even in the hard, desperate and dark stories, He takes me by the hand and leads me through. And so I will be brave with my words; I will go first. You won't find me arguing over theology within these pages, but I will tell you time and again about my Jesus.

It is my joy to know you are holding in your hands words that have been much prayed over, and it is a delight to offer a gift to you amongst the pages: prints designed by talented artists, created with you in mind. To find out how you can download each of the designs as a free print, make sure to read "a gift for you" at the end of the book.

If you've been a regular reader at my blog over the years, you may recognize a few repurposed blog posts that were key writings through many of the different ampersand seasons of my life. Even though some of the words may be familiar, they are only a small piece that lay the groundwork for a grander story God has been writing all along.

The truth is, there is much of life that I have yet to live. I suspect that as time goes on I will look back over these words and wonder at how I could have said so and so or left such and such out. But this is what I know today, these are the things that I believe to be true, and this is the story that He has given me to tell with my life.

We live in the tension of the Already and the Not Yet. I have been redeemed; I am being redeemed. I am made new; I am being made new. We belong to the Kingdom but for now, we are all just walking each other home.

Wherever you are in the tension, whatever page you find yourself on, it is my hope and prayer that you will meet Jesus in between these pages as you navigate your own in between season.

with so much love,
kait

introduction

I cry almost every time I see an ampersand.

And yes, it's just as awkward and unfortunate as you're imagining.

It doesn't matter if that little symbol shows up in a lettered quote on my Instagram feed or on a highway billboard, I immediately start blinking back tears.

An ampersand connects two different thoughts or ideas. It goes right in the middle and keeps the story going. Essentially, an ampersand is the symbol for the word "and."

When you see an ampersand you know the story isn't over just yet.

That right there, that one idea, is why I love ampersands so much.

My story isn't over.

Your story isn't over.

May we never forget.

Every time I see that little symbol I whisper, either out loud or deep down in my soul, the words that you see on the cover of this book.

Even if not.

I first came across that short phrase as I was reading the book of Daniel. In chapter 3, three guys named Hananiah, Mishael, and Azariah were faced with a difficult situation. You might know them as

Shadrach, Meshach, and Abednego. They were exiles in Babylon, taken from their families, their homeland, and everything they called familiar. Even their names were stripped away in an effort to force them to assimilate to a new culture, leaving behind the people they once were and the faith they claimed.

The king at that time, Nebuchadnezzer, built a gold statue that was ninety feet high. It was set up on the Dura plain, and so picture with me a vastness that you wouldn't find anywhere near a major city. Think "the middle of no where" and you're on the right track. And then, smack in the middle of nowhere, there is a statue as tall as a nine-story building.

King Neb, because I happen to think nicknames are totally fair game when your name is Nebuchadnezzer, ordered everybody who was anybody to come celebrate the dedication of the statue, which would be used as an idol in worship. Almost every celebration has music of some kind, and this was no exception. King Neb had a band ready to play — trumpets, trombones, tubas and baritones, drums and cymbals — and the people were ordered to fall to their knees in worship as soon as the music began.

And then the kicker — anyone who refused to kneel in worship would immediately be thrown alive into a roaring furnace.

No big deal.

Casual, really.

The band started and every person, regardless of race, color or creed, fell to their knees and worshiped the golden statue.

Well, almost everyone. It turns out three guys kept standing. After King Neb was notified, he ordered

Shadrach, Meshach, and Abednego to be brought in. Furious, he asked them if what he heard was true. Before they could answer, he offered them a second chance. The band would play again and they would either fall to their knees in worship or be pitched into a roaring furnace, no questions asked. The king ended his rant with eleven words that form a hypothetical question that God intended to answer:

"Who is the god who can rescue you from my power?"

There is no indication that the men took a moment to consult with one another about a game plan, no hemming and hawing or talking around the question left hanging in the air. Instead, they replied, "Nebuchadnezzar, we have no need to defend our actions in this matter. We are ready for the test. If you throw us into the blazing furnace, then the God we serve is able to rescue us from a furnace of blazing fire and release us from your power, Your Majesty. *But even if He does not,* O king, you can be sure that we still will not serve your gods and we will not worship the golden statue you erected."[1]

I can't help but also include these verses, so blunt and almost humorous, in The Message version:

"Your threat means nothing to us. If you throw us in the fire, the God we serve can rescue us from your roaring furnace and anything else you might cook up, O king. *But even if he doesn't,* it wouldn't make a bit of difference, O king. We still wouldn't serve your gods or worship the gold statue you set up."[2]

Even if not...

Even if you honor your threat and throw us to the flames.

Even if your guards take us away and set us on fire.

5

Even if you change your mind and punish us another way.

Even if the Lord chooses not to deliver us.

Even if we're pitched into the furnace, live to tell the tale, and you throw something else our way.

Even then, we will serve Him. Even then, we will only worship His name. Even then, we will still declare that He is good. Even then, we will refuse to fall for an idol because we have already fallen for the only One worthy of our devotion.

Will He rescue us? Oh, we hope so. Will we trust Him to be with us and to see us through? Absolutely. But just so you know, O king, while our God is fully capable of rescuing us from any punishment you come up with, He might see fit to allow things to continue as you have planned. Not for our harm, but for our good.

And so, O king, we have to tell you that we believe our God will come through in a way that will spare our lives. And yet even if not, we will still refuse to kneel because we choose to yield to His ways. No matter what the cost, we will live our lives as a sacrifice.

Can't you see King Neb's face purple with rage? He ordered the furnace to be cranked up seven times hotter than usual. You know, just in case an already blazing hot furnace wouldn't be enough to kill the men. And then with hands and feet bound, Shadrach, Meshach, and Abednego were thrown into the roaring fire. Daniel 3:19 says that the furnace was so hot that the men who carried Shadrach, Meshach, and Abednego were killed from the heat of the scorching flames.

And yet when King Neb looked into the furnace, likely expecting to see a swirl of orange and yellow swallowing the men alive, he saw four men walking freely about, completely unharmed.

He questioned whether they had been bound, and honestly I have to pause to laugh because really, is that your greatest concern? How about the fourth man? How about how they are still alive in a roaring furnace? No? The ropes, really? But he had to see for himself and so he went to the door of the roaring furnace and called out "Shadrach, Meshach, and Abednego, servants of the High God, come out here!"[3]

The three men walked right out of the fire without a single hair singed, no scorch marks on their clothing, and not even the smell of fire lingering on their skin. This right here is a miracle because have you ever been camping? Or, better yet, have you burnt popcorn in the microwave and then opened the steaming bag? Just the smoke that is released into the air from that one bag of blackened popcorn will get all over you within seconds.

But these guys, who were walking around in a blazing hot furnace, didn't even remotely smell of smoke.

King Neb recognized the true God through their actions and their willingness to lay their own lives on the line. Then he issued this decree: "Anyone anywhere, of any race, color, or creed, who says anything against the God of Shadrach, Meshach, and Abednego will be ripped to pieces, limb from limb, and their houses torn down. There has never been a god who can pull off a rescue like that."[4]

He wasn't one for doling out minor punishments,

I'll give him that. But don't you love that last line, those words about the Hero of the story?

There has never been a god who can pull off a rescue like that.

From our perspective, the story is wrapped up like a gift with a beautiful bow on top. But in the moment, right then and there? The men didn't know how the story would end. There wasn't an assurance that King Neb, and therefore the entire country, would see the truth because three guys dared to say "even if not." But they said — and lived out — those words anyway because they trusted the Author of the story.

Those three little words are guaranteed to change your story but they'll also change the lives of those around you.

What hangs in the balance of your "even if not"? Whose eyes will remain closed, whose story unchanged?

I know it, trust me I do, that those can be three of the hardest words to say. Maybe that's why I whisper them to myself and to my friend Jesus with every glimpse of an ampersand.

I've had my "even if not" moments, but that doesn't mean there won't be other opportunities for me to declare it again. Every day this world asks you to bow down and bend your knees to the glitz, the glam, the stats and the lies.

Don't fall for it.

Literally, please do not fall.

Every single day you're handed one million little opportunities to worship, but it's your choice which god you'll fall for — the world or the One who made the world.

I'm convinced many of us are living in the ampersand, in an in between place that is crying out in both pain and belief that God will use the hurt. We're desperate for Him to come through, desperate for this to not be the end. Surely the story can't end this way, right? God will come through, I promise you that. But you and I both know it deep down in our souls, whether we're ready to admit it or not: God *is* going to come through but it might not look like what we're hoping for.

It is in that place that we whisper the words again and again and again, even when they are more a prayer of "Lord, I believe; help my unbelief."

Even if not. Even if not. Even if not.

I have found myself on both ends of the spectrum, in the dark and in the light, lonely and surrounded by community, broken and mended. But the truth is, most of life is lived somewhere in between. Most of us are in the ampersand, but just so you know — you'll find God there, too.

Every story is different and every story matters. My story, as you'll read in these pages, holds a whole lot of brokenness, unfulfilled dreams, and four years of praying the same prayer while seeing nary a change for the better.

Four years of prayers, four years of offering up "even if not," four years of hoping against hope and waiting when the days stretched into weeks and the months into years. Four years of a chapter I didn't want included in my story, and yet God can be found on those pages, too.

Whether you don't think your story matters or you

believe it does, and that's why you're so scared that this is how the story ends, I get it. I've been there, and truthfully I find myself flipping back to those pages every so often. But not today. Not this time. It's time to turn the page, to live in the next chapter, to declare over it all, every sentence and every moment, that God is the One writing the story and He doesn't need a pencil with an eraser because He won't make a mistake.

We believe, Lord, that You are more than capable of rescue. This is not too big for You. And with the very same lips that declare Your might, we also acknowledge that Your rescue might not look like what we hope for. Even if not, Lord, we say with one voice, even if it shakes as the words slip out, that we trust Your plan. You hold the pen, our lives are the stories, and in the middle of all this mess we still choose to believe You are writing a masterpiece.

the first step to receiving an answer is to be brave enough to ask a question

Chapter One

questions & answers

Christ alone is the substance of our hope, the truth on which we rely. Hardship will invade our world and miracles may or may not come, but in every circumstance Jesus will always be Christ. That truth is enough to create faith that can withstand anything. // Mike Nappa, God In Slow Motion

I am the spitting image of my mother. There's no doubt about it, I am hers. This is not something I question. She is my mom, my friend, and my hero. I get my stubborn streak, my wide feet, and my thick brown hair from her. Unfortunately she didn't pass down her voice, although her love for music and singing found its way into my bones. She did, however, always encourage me to dream big.

As I grew up, my childhood dreams began to change ever so slowly. While I didn't question my relationship with my mother, I began to question many things about the world around me.

At the same time, I began to dream big dreams that would take me on my own path, away from my mom and all that was familiar. Dreams that would push me to doubt and wonder, only to discover that the answer I was searching for was there all along.

They say that Florida is part of the South but I'm here to tell you that isn't the case. Geographically, yes, Floridians call home a piece of land that does, in fact, find itself located in the lower Eastern part of the United States. But South Florida? It is northern through and through.

Sweet tea is not a thing, football is not a religion, and I never heard the words "yes ma'am" or "no sir." As a whole, we are impolite, hurried, and we enjoy wearing flip-flops on Christmas. Love it or hate it, South Floridian culture is like living in New York — if you just take out the snow and flashing lights and add in the beach.

For the first eighteen years of my life, that culture was my home. I legitimately thought I lived in the South although I kept hearing talk of something called a Bible Belt. I mean, we had Coca-Cola in our refrigerator. What more could be necessary?

But then I moved to Alabama.

You could say my eyes were opened.

First of all, there's an accent here. A 'twang, if you will. People drink dirt water, which they refer to as sweet tea, as if their very lives depend on it. If I'm driving along the interstate and I need to change lanes, people actually slow down to let me over.

This is game changing.

South Floridians will speed up just so you can't switch lanes, as if driving is one big Xbox race. And can we talk about the interstates real fast? There are stoplights here.

On the interstate.

As you're driving.

Please tell me this isn't normal elsewhere. I had never even heard of such and so you best believe I was completely floored to find myself coming to a complete stop for a red light on the interstate.

I've been here four years this month and I still shake my head and a laugh quietly slips out when I come to a stop on the highway. But somewhere in those four years, Alabama changed me.

And I don't just mean that I now say "y'all" on a daily basis. No, Alabama changed me.

South Florida gave me questions but Alabama helped me ask them. South Florida raised me and then Alabama gave me wings to fly.

This is the place where I found my people and the place I wrestled with the dark. Here is where I found the courage to doubt my doubts and listen to my questions. Alabama is where I learned to take what I had been taught and use it in "the real world." It's where I walked my own path and learned to fly in the process. It's where I found the sweet spot between being my mother's daughter and my own person. It's the place where I realized love is a risk worth taking.

Alabama is where I discovered that it's okay to question as long I always come back to the Answer.

Many situations provide an either/or option. Either we can eat out for dinner or we can stay in. Either you're the type of person who makes your bed every morning or you're not. Either you view reading as an enjoyable activity or a cruel punishment.

Sometimes, though, life is more of a both/and.

You can walk in the darkness and believe in the light. There are seasons that make you want to crawl back in bed and hide from the noise, and yet you feel the pull to set out on a new adventure. You can't decide which pull is greater and so it's *both* and it's *and*.

There is so much noise everywhere we turn. A quick glance at your Facebook feed, Twitter stream, or news station can more than overwhelm a person. Add in books and people and everywhere more words and, well, the world has become mighty loud.

I haven't always right known what to say. Do I need to say anything? Do I even have something worth saying? Should I wait until all my questions are answered before I add to the noise?

For a while I pulled back. Way back. I tried saying no to hanging out with friends and said yes to laying my head down an hour earlier each night. I was careful with my commitments and I tried to slow down.

I've attempted to pause but the world kept on spinning mad. And my world kept on spinning with it.

Without a word I said to the world, "Hey, if you need me, I'll be the one hiding under the covers. You keep doing your thing and I'll just hang out right here. In the dark. In the quiet. Let me know when you've got some answers for me and I'll come out into the light of day."

But the truth of the matter is that we can't wait until we've got all the answers to start fully living. We can't hide from our questions because then we also, in turn, hide from the answers.

Most of us are living in the middle of the story. We don't fully understand where we've been and we sure don't know where we're going. We are living in the ampersand of it all, in the place between our questions and answers, and if some of us got real honest, we would admit that we have questions that keep us up at night and chase after us in the daylight.

Truthfully, sometimes that's why we hide. We're so scared to ask the questions because we're terrified of what the answers might be. Or maybe we're even more scared that there won't be an answer at all.

And so we sit in the dark and we search for a flashlight, making finger-puppet shadow-dances under the covers. But you and I both know that isn't enough, not forever.

In a both/and life, you've got an either/or decision. Either you ask your questions or you suffer in silence. Either you pull the covers over your face and whimper from the noise or you dare to get up and get at it for one more day.

I had a lot of questions. I had one hundred different wonderings and no idea how to begin to voice them. There have been months of bags under my eyes from nightmares and a constant sadness that couldn't be explained. Years of questioning my place and doubting love existed convinced me to pull the covers up real tight around my face. The words in this book will tell the journey of how I learned to say "I trust You, even if not" when it was dark, I was lonely, and I couldn't see past my present circumstances.

For now you simply need to know I get it. I have been where you are, sitting in that place full of questions but too worried to voice a single one. And you need to know that I still have questions. The difference is that now I know where to take them.

At some point I started to peer out, peeking my head above the sheets and then slowly dipping my toes into the shallow end of a spinning world.

Sometimes our questions take the form of "What should I eat for breakfast?" or "Should I start a new episode on Netflix even though it's already one in the morning?"

Those questions have answers.

But sometimes our questions look more like this:

- What if I don't get a miracle?
- Should I stay or should I go?
- Am I enough? Am I too much?
- Is there someone out there for me?
- Does God hear me?
- Do I begin something new or give more to what already is?
- Is it too late? Is it too early?
- Does love really exist?
- Why is there evil in the world?
- Can God handle all these questions?

And that's just the tip of the iceberg of questions I've raised to the heavens.

Through my own questioning and doubting I've come to find that the first step to receiving an answer is being brave enough to ask a question.

Sometimes that bravery simply looks like being willing to wait and listen in the dark. Because He will answer, I can promise you that. Spoiler alert: He is the Answer.

The truth is, every question finds its answer rooted in the same place, all running together and connected to the same tree. We just have to make sure we take our questions to the right Source.

2,000 years ago a tree was split and a man named Jesus spilt His blood on that piece of wood placed into the ground. And every single time you ask your questions, whether you yell them at the sky or whisper them quietly, if you look to that tree you'll find the Answer.

It may not be an audible response. You may not see a message in the clouds. Personally, I've never experienced more than a gentle tug, a quiet knowing in my soul.

Sometimes, perhaps most of the time, the only answer I receive is that He is the Answer.

On my best days, that's more than enough. On my worst, I want to close the blinds, grab a pint of ice cream and climb back in bed. But those are the times where I've found Him to be the most present, the strongest kind of faithful. Those are the times He asks me to say "even if not." In the doubts and the darkness, in the wondering and the wandering, He keeps on showing up. He keeps on being the Answer.

Sometimes He answers my questions with a question and that's just the worst. If you slow down enough you'll likely hear Him asking you, too.

"Will you trust Me, love? Will you believe Me enough

and trust that I am good, even if I don't answer your questions? When everything is dark and you don't know which way to turn, will you cling to Me and listen only for My voice? I will be here. I will choose you. Will you choose Me?"

He may answer our questions, but even if not we have the Answer above all answers. And the truth is, even when we don't have all the answers we so long for, we don't actually need to know the future. We just need to trust the One who authors it into being.

I heard once that God is the One who overcomes and because He does, we can come over.

I haven't always understood what that meant, and yet I cling to this promise when the noise gets louder and life gets crazier. When bills are stacking up, a relationship is falling apart, and sickness enters into the picture. When life is topsy-turvy and spinning a bit out of control, when it feels like I'm carrying the weight of the world on my shoulders, and when my hands are full.

Even then, I can come over because there is One who has overcome. The overcoming part sounded great but frankly, if I'm "coming over" then I wanted to know where I was going.

In the Old Testament, there was a curtain in the temple that separated the people from the Holy of Holies, which is where the Lord chose to dwell. You and I, we would not have been able to enter into His presence. The curtain would have separated us — not from His love, but from His beautiful, consuming, powerful presence.

But when Jesus Christ died as a sacrifice, the curtain that kept the distance and created a separation was torn in two from top to bottom.[1] It was nothing man could do, but God did it for man. He entered into our mess and invited us into His presence. Now we can come over because He has overcome. He was the Answer to the problem we didn't even know we had.

The world that feels like it's on your shoulders is really in His more than capable hands. So maybe we simply hold onto hope and choose to believe it's not really about knowing all the answers but trusting the Answer. Maybe we choose to believe He's got it all figured out and His plans are so very good. Maybe we keep on asking our questions in His presence because the veil was torn and we can enter in.

I believe that even with all our questions and uncertainties and doubts we don't know how to put words to, we'll find there is a certainty and an assurance of who He is. We'll find a ripped veil and a kept promise that His goodness hasn't gone anywhere, even when the only answer to be found is Him.

This curtain-tearing God does not abandon His people. He does not walk away. He does not unchoose us. He is not staring down at us from heaven and tapping His foot, checking His watch to see just how long it'll take us to figure this whole 'life' thing out. Instead, He is patiently waiting and quietly longing to be the safe place we run to in the dark, the quiet we enter into when the noise of the world is blaring in our ears, the balm to our scars and the healing for our hurts.

He never promised to answer all our questions, but He promised to be the Answer to every question we'll ever face.

Sometimes we get so caught up in figuring out the future that we can't focus in the present. There's a time and a place for planning, but if we miss today then what's the point in worrying about tomorrow? Time spent worrying today is time taken away from praying for the very things that cause us to worry. And there's no room for worrying when you're busy worshipping.

I doubt anyone 2,000 years ago was praying for the curtain to be torn. They weren't worried about entering into the Lord's presence because they simply trusted He would go with them. But He wanted to *be* with them.

We can't plan for how God is going to move or work in our lives, but we can plan on Him doing so. We can come over and raise our hands instead of making our plans and to-do lists for tomorrow. We can consciously choose not to question Him, but to speak our questions in His presence.

He is the One who overcomes and so now we can come over.

There are some things in life that I just don't question, like being the daughter of Jimmy and Kim

Bouchillon. That's who I am and I know it. There are other things I've questioned and received answers to, like staying in Alabama after graduating college.

But then there are those questions we ask that will likely never receive an answer on this side of heaven. God is good but this earth holds so much evil and sometimes our worlds are just dark.

Sometimes the enemy attacks and we are left wounded and bleeding. Sometimes there isn't an explanation for any of it, even when we know God hasn't gone anywhere. The veil was torn; He is with us. But life still holds some hard questions.

I'll be honest with you, "it happens to the best of us" is both trite and inaccurate. Sometimes it just plain happens and it's just plain hard. Sometimes it can feel like a season of groping in the dark, hands straight out in front of you, searching aimlessly for the light switch.

But this is what I know and this is what I am sure of: He is the light of the world. We don't have to walk in darkness because we have the Light with us at all times.[2] What the enemy means for evil can be turned for our good.[3]

It *will* be turned for our good.

He is always faithful. This promise-keeping, all-knowing, forever-loving God who has the answer to every question, who *is* the Answer to every question, made a covenant with you.

In the Old Testament the most secure covenant was a blood covenant. This particular type of covenant was made by splitting animals in half and laying them in two rows on the ground. The two people entering into the covenant would then grasp hands and walk between the bloody animal pieces together. It sounds gross and absolutely disgusting because it is.

But it was meant to signify that if one person didn't uphold their side of the covenant, they were essentially saying "may it be done to me as it was to these animals."

So if you feel the need to make a blood covenant with someone for any reason, you best make sure you're serious about what you're committing to.

When God entered into a covenant with Abram in Genesis 15, He first put Abram to sleep. And then while Abram slept, God promised both sides of the bargain. In His promise-keeping, all-knowing, forever-loving way, He knew we would never be able to keep our promise. We would fail, we would falter, and we would never uphold our side. The penalty would be ours to pay.

And so God promised. Both sides. And then He paid the penalty. Jesus came, His body broke, and the veil was split in two. He broke so that all things could be made new.

He is a promise-keeping God to a promise-breaking people.

He was there at the beginning, He's with us in the in between, and He knows what's coming.

He is working in each season, even when the world is noisy and there are no answers written in the sky. That still, small voice is present and active. We are more than conquerors in Christ, through Christ, and with Christ. Even when we are conquerors with questions.

And so we must doubt our doubts and hold them up to the Light. He is the Truth and He is the Answer and so we quietly hand our questions over, choosing to believe that He will be enough even if the only answer we receive is Him.

Hold onto what you know is true in the light when you cannot see it in the dark. And if there comes a time when your grip loosens and you feel yourself falling, rest in knowing this promise-keeping God has got you tight and sure. He will be a safe place for your questions.

It's okay to question, but just remember you already have the Answer.

all is well

Chapter Two

sickness & healing

I give you all the credit, God — you got me out of that mess.
God, my God, I yelled for help and you put me together. God,
you pulled me out of the grave, gave me another chance at life
when I was down-and-out. // Psalm 30:1-3, The Message

I never would have written a brain tumor into my story but I would never wish to write it out.

It was a part of me and now it is a part of my story, one I never expected to have and now have the gift of telling for the rest of my days. You could pass me in the grocery store aisles or sit one table over at the coffee shop and you would never know that I had brain surgery at age seventeen. For a long time we didn't have any answers and to this day I simply refer to those months as when I was "sick." But flashback to a Saturday in February of 2010 and you'll see that the story had turned to a new chapter overnight, one I didn't yet know I was in.

We thought it was food poisoning.
I woke up to an empty house on a quiet Saturday

morning and immediately knew something was wrong. I've never been a runner but I sprinted to the bathroom like my life depended on it. And then I proceeded to throw up until I fell asleep at night.

It's just as glamorous as it sounds, really. I sat next to the toilet and threw up again and again until my body wearily fell asleep around midnight. Although I was exhausted when I woke the next morning, everything had returned to normal. Life went on and we didn't question it. But over the course of the next six weeks, this episode would repeat itself four more times.

Blood tests didn't show anything to be concerned about and because of how the sickness was playing out, I couldn't make it to the doctor when I was ill. Quite frankly, I was happy if I could just make it to the bathroom. And so my mom and I would drive to the doctor's office the following day and explain what had happened.

After multiple visits, the doctor said it was all in my head and I was making everything up. That's only slightly funny because in a way, it actually was all in my head.

Months went by and the episodes, as I've grown to call them, slowed down. One month would be terrible and then weeks would go by without any cause for concern. In May I was given medication for vertigo but that didn't make a difference. That's probably because I didn't have vertigo.

By the time the calendar flipped to June I was almost used to being sick, as strange as that is to say. But when I came home from a mission trip to Jamaica and could no longer move my neck in any direction, my parents and I knew something was very, very wrong.

We were finally able to talk with the main doctor at the practice, and I inwardly praised the Lord that we wouldn't have to see the doctor who thought I just wanted attention. For the first time in months, it felt like a doctor might actually take me seriously. He listened attentively, reviewed my records, and then gave me the option of getting either an MRI or a spinal tap.

Now, to be fair, I am not a doctor. But I've seen my fair share of Grey's Anatomy and so this wasn't even a question. Should you ever be presented with these two choices, choose the MRI. Every time, choose the MRI.

And so on an otherwise normal Tuesday evening at the tail end of June, I found myself putting on a flimsy gown and lying completely still inside a machine. That was unusual enough.

Stranger still was this hope stirring inside and a quiet prayer that went a little something like this: *God, please let them find something. Let it be easily fixable, but please let them find something. I'm desperate for an answer.*

Little did I know He was going to answer that prayer with an opportunity to say an "even if not" that would shape the rest of my days.

The following morning we got the call to come to

the doctor's office immediately. A few hours later I wrote these words on my blog:

Apparently, it's time for a little heart-to-heart — one that I wasn't expecting to have.

There's no easy way to say this, so let me just dive in. Remember that MRI I had last night? Well I was planning to tell you all about it today. I was going to tell you how freezing cold the room was, how nice the lady was, and how it all went well. I was going to explain that we wouldn't know the results until Thursday morning when I went to see the doctor. I planned to say once again that I was hoping and praying for answers that would be fixable. Easily fixable.

I have answers now.

Not all the answers, but the MRI showed what's been causing me to feel such horrible neck pain as well as why I've gotten so dizzy and thrown up so much.

I have a brain tumor.

Mom and I went to the doctor earlier this afternoon because he didn't want to wait until tomorrow. We don't know much about it except that the tumor must be operated on as soon as possible. I will have surgery within the next few days.

I plan to come back to the house I call home. I love Him and I know where I'll go if He calls me to that heavenly home, but I'm not ready to go there yet. I have so much more life that I want to live.

Please know that I'm not that scared. God already knew this would happen. He knows how long the tumor has been there and He knows if it's cancerous or not.

No matter what happens, I trust Him completely.

If I didn't have Him, I don't know how I'd be doing through all of this. It's not what we were expecting to hear today, but we're going to be aggressive and get this thing out.

He's my Healer and I trust Him regardless of what happens.[1]

I should probably clear things up by saying that I still look back on those words and shake my head in disbelief. I am the last person you would expect to be "okay" in that situation. The most logical and expected reaction for a seventeen-year-old receiving that news would be to fall apart. And yet I have never felt such absolute and complete peace in my entire life.

There were no worries. There were no doubts. I couldn't think of a single reason to be scared. The only thing I felt was peace. I was more than okay, but by the grace of God.

Although the news that met me on that Wednesday morning would alter my life forever, it had no effect on my eternal destination. And so while all was not whole on earth, all was still well.

I knew He could choose to heal me, but I believed God would still be God and He would still be good, even if not.

Two days later we met with my neurosurgeon and on Tuesday morning, exactly one week after having my first MRI, I found myself sitting in a car driving away from home, praying that I would return.

It was July 6, 2010.

During the early morning hours of July 8, I had what we will kindly refer to as a 'friendly discussion' with God.

Surgery went smoothly, the tumor was completely removed, and we would receive test results answering all cancer-related questions in a few weeks.

I was transferred to a new room and as I tried to sleep in between the every-twenty-minute-check-ins from the nurses on night shift, I had two separate dreams where I greatly sensed God's presence inside the dream.

I don't know if it all actually works that way and please don't hear me say I went to heaven or anything like that. I hesitate to even include this and the truth is, I was pumped full of medication at the time. But I remember it clearly to this day and so perhaps there is some weight to the story.

Both dreams were short, the second a continuation of the first. I found myself lying at the bottom of a shallow, wooden boat. Instead of sitting atop ocean waves, the boat was swaying gently back and forth in mid-air. As the boat slowly began to rise, I had a growing sensation that the higher we went, the further from earth I was.

For reasons I'll never be able to explain in human words, inside that dream I believed with absolute certainty that He was gently carrying me home to heaven.

But I didn't want to go, not yet. It started as a whisper and I grew louder and louder as I begged Him to let me stay. Over and over I asked for just a little more time. I wanted to be with Him in heaven but there was something so deep inside that kept pulling at me, tugging me back and saying that the story wasn't over yet. And so I asked Him to keep writing.

I woke up, blinking quickly in an effort to rid the sleep from my heavy eyelids, eyes darting back and forth to see where I was. Still in the hospital bed, I breathed a sigh of relief and slipped back into the dream. This time the boat was still moving side to side but it slowly lowered until it came to rest on the water.

On July 8, 2010, I woke up with the deepest assurance that my story wasn't over but I couldn't waste a single day I had been given. Every single day is truly a gift of grace.

As summer came to a close, we received the news that I was cancer-free. Just seeing those words typed in black against the white screen, it all feels like too much, as if the gift is just too great to hold in my hands.

He didn't have to heal me.

He didn't have to write healing into my days.

He didn't have to lower the boat.

I would have loved Him just as much if the boat kept going skyward. He would have been just as good if senior year included chemotherapy and radiation, and yet He chose to write a different story with my days.

I will never understand it but I will forever thank Him.

I long to carry this story well. I want my history to be His legacy, my life shining only one Name. He has healed me in more ways than one and the scar on the back of my head only tells a piece of the story.

And so now this is mine to carry. This is my story. It isn't pretty all the way through. It is confusing and unfair and gracious and mine. It is mine to tell and mine to live. It is my responsibility to share and testify that my body was broken and now I am healed.

My brain used to hold a tumor. Now the scans show fluid in the shape of a heart right there where the tumor was. Only God could make that happen, leaving a reminder just for me that He is the Healer of all our troubles.

This is my story. Oh, may it be my theme in glory. That He binds up the brokenhearted. That He heals the deepest wounds, loves the ugliest hurts, and instead of walking away He walks through.

Through the dark of night, through the questions and wonderings and wanderings and doubts, He carries you right through because He is love and light and always, no matter what, good.

Even when your story holds a chapter that contains a brain tumor. Even then.

Maybe especially then.

Human hands worked to assist in a miracle that was all God's doing. There have been other scares and more MRI's than I ever wished to have. I've been poked and prodded and put under. Several years later, pain still creeps in and the scar throbs but it is only a reminder of what once was.

There are countless tests and scans of my brain and they all tell the same story over and over again: I was sick and I have been healed.

But that story was already mine long before an early July morning rid me of a brain tumor.

My soul knew the truth: He could heal me but I would choose to love Him even if not. And if He chose not to heal me? It would not make Him any less of a healer.

The truth is, my history includes a chapter titled July 6, 2010, but it's actually His Story. I just get to tell it.

Although I'm grateful to live each day soaking it all in — the smell of grass and the sound of a baby's laugh, and all of the countless little things I never want to take for granted again — when I'm real honest there are days that I struggle with it all.

I wrestle with the fact that I'm alive and countless others with the same diagnosis are not.

Years later, I still walk the hospital halls at every checkup, purposely looking at the faces of the children and parents sitting in the waiting room with fish and coral made out of painted handprints, praying they would ultimately receive the same news that I did.

Soon after surgery, I began to wrestle with the question of why. With every piece of me, I was grateful. And with every piece of me, I asked "why me?"

Why was I healed and not someone else? Why do little children have to experience the deep physical pain that I went through?

I remember lying in the hospital bed and hearing a little child screaming one room over. Even while believing it doesn't work this way, I thanked Him over and over for allowing me to carry a brain tumor instead of a young child, one who couldn't understand what was happening. I whispered it to Him again and again, "At least I understand why this hurts. Oh, all these littles that I pass in the hallways — how can they understand the throbbing inside? Thank You that it's me. Thank You that it's me. Thank You that it's me."

I whisper it again every time I return.

When I was teaching my legs to walk again after being horizontal for days, I made it around the nurses' desk and was doing my best to go all the way down the hall. As I went to turn left, I moved over to avoid walking into a little boy on my right. His entire head was covered in gauze and I could barely keep from throwing up, much less keep the tears from leaking and my feet moving.

He was so very little.

I've carried with me the pain and the healing, the wonderings and the gratefulness, and all of it is mixed together into the story He has given me to share. I don't know why He chose to write this into my history and I surely cannot understand all the "whys," but I know beyond a shadow of a doubt that I trust the One who is writing every story.

Even the story of the little boy on the right side of the hallway.

I will never see him again but every time I walk those halls I pray for the ones waiting for results and asking for healing. Sometimes there is nothing to do but pray.

I may never know why a golf-ball sized tumor was written into the pages of my story. You may never receive healing in the way you're requesting or answers to the questions that keep you up into the early morning hours.

Sometimes the only answer is that this is how He has authored the pages.

Whatever day you find yourself reading these words, can I tell you that He is faithful? Nothing about who He is hangs in the balance of what story this page will tell.

He has already won. The story is already written. We must make the choice to trust the One holding the pen, believing that He will heal and trusting Him even if not.

He isn't taken aback by your brokenness. It is not too much for Him. He is the Answer you may not even know you're searching for and all those broken pieces, all the hurting and thin places, He will heal and mend. It's what He does; it's who He is.

When we let God
do the mending
BROKEN THINGS
can become
BLESSED THINGS

Chapter Three
broken & mended

*Of one thing I am perfectly sure:
God's story never ends with 'ashes.' // Elisabeth Elliot*

The word *community* has gotten a lot of hype recently. Some have argued that it is overused and I'd like to offer that it is instead undervalued. But you know what they say — you never know a good thing until it's gone.

I've been without community. I have watched friends walk away and I've seen the Body of Christ break in two. There is no story harder to tell, no chapter that hurts more to revisit and talk about, than this one. The scar from brain surgery is an outward sign of a body broken, but the scars left behind from broken community can't be seen until you dig down deep. Nothing has cut so deeply, nothing has bruised me black and blue, like the wounds of community.

In the months following surgery, I had countless people express kind words in some form of "You have been so brave!" What they didn't know is that I had already lived through my worst nightmare one year earlier. And then I spent the next set of three hundred and sixty-five days walking with my friend

Jesus.

I wasn't brave. I just knew He wouldn't leave.

There is a prophet in the Bible named Ezekiel and I feel safe saying he was one strange dude. Feel free to check out Ezekiel 4 and 5 for a few stories that will leave you shaking your head.

Chapter 37 takes us to a scene where Ezekiel has been carried away by the Spirit of the Lord to a valley filled with dry bones. There was nothing beautiful to look at. No matter which direction he turned, there was no sign of life left to be found. The Bible says that the bones were completely dried out, bleached by the heat of the sun, and yes, they probably smelled.

Try to imagine yourself standing there. As far as your eyes can see, dead bones are piled atop one another, limbs sticking out in every direction. You are all alone. The breath of life has literally been sucked out and all that remains is carnage.

It may not be that hard to imagine. You may have found yourself in this valley before, whether it be because of a relationship ending, a financial decision, a job loss, a health report or countless other scenarios.

When it's just you and Jesus and a valley of dry bones, what then?

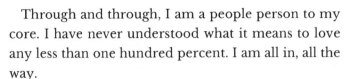

Through and through, I am a people person to my core. I have never understood what it means to love any less than one hundred percent. I am all in, all the way.

My biggest fear has nothing to do with jumping from a tall building. My worst nightmare is not a shark attack or of being sucked into a tornado. More than anything else I am terrified of being alone.

But that is exactly where I found myself in 2009. I tell you the year because it wasn't until 2013 that the dry bones began to shake with life.

There was a lot of walking in between. A whole lot of prophesying to what appeared deader than dead, days when all I could manage was to hope for hope, and years of prayers that felt unanswered.

1,596 days of declaring and whispering "even if not." This is not the story I wanted to live. And yet this is my very favorite story to tell.

Not because there's a happy ending and not because God came through in a way that blows my mind, although He did, but because my history is His Story.

I cannot sign my name to this one. I was Ezekiel, looking at the remains of what used to be life. A character on the pages, I've got nothing to do with how this story turned out. But I had a front row seat and can I tell you straight up, nothing has ruined me, changed me, shattered every promise and stolen every dream like this story. And yet the very story that broke me is the story that mended me.

I know what it's like to watch everyone walk away and find that Jesus is still there. I know what it's like to find that He and only He is enough. I've cried the buckets of tears and muffled the sobs so no one would hear. I've walked the hallways and tried to smile when all I could see were dry bones silently passing me by.

I don't know what your valley is, but this was mine.

When your Jesus-loving, God-fearing community walks away and you can barely wipe your face before more tears roll down and when the floor has imprints of your knees from so many moments when you just couldn't get back up, there is no circled date or calendar count-down that brings hope for when you'll easily breathe again.

But in the middle of years of saying "even if not," I found that I wasn't alone in the valley. He didn't drop me off there to join the dead. His love never fails, never ends, never walks away, never closes the door, never gives up, never tires, and never ever leaves you alone. His love will carry you through your darkest night.

When the world runs out He runs in. When your heart may burst open wide, His love fills the holes. When you've forgotten how to breathe He will pour in joy like oxygen.

Those years, as painful and uprooted as they were, hold some of the sweetest times. Not because things were happy or I felt known deep inside, but because He was my safe place and my roots sunk into Him. It was ugly and bitter and painful, but sometimes the skeletons hanging in your closest become the dry bones that teach you how to dance.

I had Him and only Him and He showed me day after day, hour by hour, just what faithfulness looks like.

When you abide with the Truth you'll find yourself dwelling in His goodness. He is the One who doesn't run out, run away, or run down a list of how you haven't measured up. But oh, He does run. He runs straight to you, arms open wide, love pouring out.

He is our safe place and our stories are secure in Him.

But our friend Jesus isn't much for walls and He wasn't a big fan of the ones I built. I was calloused, bruised, and torn up on the inside, but He took on flesh to bandage my wounds. He entered into the mess, determined to write a message that would show just what kind of friend He is. My greatest test has become my testimony, my messiest mess my message.

I'm a date person. It was a Tuesday afternoon, May 26, 2009, when my world imploded. My best friend and I said words that can never be taken back, like trying to put the toothpaste back in the tube.

We did it, both of us. We broke the Body of Christ and life moved on but my heart never did. I spent the next four years praying, begging, weeping, wailing, and waiting. More than anything, I prayed for reconciliation. In a valley of dry bones, I prayed for life.

And life came, but not the way I pictured it. I stared at those dry bones but they only sat there, silent and sun-scorched. Quietly, when I wasn't even looking, life blew in and love proved real. But the bones, they never moved.

He mended what broke in me but my heart-cry never changed. Did I see with my own two eyes that He is faithful and good? Did He show me in one hundred different ways that He can mend what is broken and glue back the broken pieces? One million times over, yes. He loved me at my darkest and held me at my weakest.

But still I prayed that redemption would win and that I would see reconciliation this side of heaven. Because I had already learned it long ago and I knew it true and deep, that nothing in this big wide world is impossible for Him and so why would this be too hard?

In chapter 37, Ezekiel is standing in the valley taking in his surroundings when God asks a question. Before he has a moment to question why he is where he is, God speaks. With only seven words in the English translation, God looks to see just what Ezekiel believes about God in the face of death and destruction.

"Son of man, can these bones live?"

In my own interpretation, God is asking: Am I capable? Do you believe that I can bring the dead to life? Is it possible for what seems utterly hopeless and broken to be mended back together again? Son of man, is anything impossible for Me?

A seven word question receives a five word response when Ezekiel replies, "Sovereign LORD, you alone know."

In my opinion, Ezekiel is crazy smart with his answer. His eyes see death but his heart trusts that God is God no matter the circumstance, and so he says his own version of "even if not." *Could* God do it? Absolutely. But *would* God bring life to the dead places? He wasn't sure.

And we get that, don't we? When we pray for a miracle but prepare for a burial. When we clock in from nine to five but spend our evenings researching how to start a nonprofit. When we meet a friend for coffee, daring to go beyond the "I'm fine's" and build a bridge instead of a wall.

God tells Ezekiel to prophesy to the bones and surely this must have felt ridiculous. Can you imagine standing over your childhood stuffed animals and speaking the Word of the Lord, expecting them to suddenly come to life and start waltzing around? But God tells him what to say and Ezekiel says it. The Mender declares, "I will make breath enter you, and you will come to life. I will attach tendons to you and make flesh come upon you and cover you with skin; I will put breath in you, and you will come to life. Then you will know that I am the Lord."[1]

As Ezekiel was prophesying there was a rattling sound as the very bones that lay in heaps came together, bone to bone. Tendons and flesh appeared and skin covered the stark white.

There was hope, but the bones were not alive. There was movement, but there was no life.

We hadn't spoken in years, this friend and I. We were doing life in circles all around each other, never with each other, and no matter how many times I prayed that God would change her heart toward us, it wasn't changing.

But He was continuing to change me. He was remaking and renewing and redeeming.

He gave me day after day and opportunity after opportunity to decide if I would declare with my mouth what my heart believed, yet my mind struggled to understand. Time and again, He asked if I would be satisfied even if not, if I would love Him even if not, if I would trust His goodness toward me even if the only thing that changed *was* me.

Some days the answer was easy. Some days it was all I could do to pray one word: Jesus.

I've never heard the word "wait" so many times and after four and a half years, quite frankly I was tired of praying for beauty from ashes and seeing nothing but a heap of black. The bones were dead. Hope was getting hard to hold onto and there were days I had to hope for hope to stick around. Because how long does it take before you pray the same prayer for what feels like a lifetime and then finally see it happen?

There was nothing happening.

For four and a half years He worked in me and in her and I kept waiting for Him to work on us.

The prayer felt too big to keep on praying, but Isaiah 43:18-19 implored me to continue looking, keep on asking, and never stop believing:

Forget the former things; do not dwell on the past. See, I am doing a new thing! Now it springs up; do you not perceive it? I am making a way in the wilderness and streams in the wasteland.

Hear me say it: He would have been good if nothing had changed. He would have been faithful if things had stayed the same. God would still be God whether He answered my prayer or not.

Even if nothing changed about my situation, nothing about my view of God would change.

But for the one struggling to hold onto hope, hear me say this too: the land of the living is a beautiful place and it is worth waiting for.

I realize that sometimes the book is closed and that in the closing, God receives the most glory. But we had a few more pages to walk, even when the story seemed long over, because God did what felt flat out impossible. I still haven't figured out how to put words to a miracle.

Lest you think it was all sunshine and rainbows, you should know that it was messy and ugly and plain hard. While I spent four years processing and healing, she simply ignored and moved on. And so when she began to process and when we chose to wade into the deep end together, it was not pretty. But it was good. It was so very good. His grace covered every difficult moment, like skin covering dried-out bones.

Those years of praying and not seeing any answers were not fruitless. God had been working away, redeeming us both individually, and it was time for reconciliation to take center stage.

He had done a work in both of us. Just as Ezekiel continued to prophesy to the breath and the bones that held together started to stand up as breath rushed through the valley, we watched the impossible become possible in front of our very eyes.

Brokenness was mended, wounds were healed and the cracks started to spill out grace.

Redemption won. Jesus won. The story of this relationship was a closed book, the Author seemingly ending the story mid-sentence. But He saw fit to pick up the pen and keep on writing. And maybe, just maybe, He never put it down in the first place. After all, there's no such thing as a wasted season.

I have never seen beauty from ashes, life from death, or light from dark quite like the story He has given us. Our lives are a living testimony that nothing is too far gone or too impossible for God. It really has nothing to do with us and everything to do with Him.

We could not heal our relationship. Two hurt people could not mend what was broken. Thank goodness for a Healer.

Sometimes strength isn't having never been broken, but about courageously growing strong in those broken places. Sometimes strength looks like seeing a valley of dry bones and believing they will be brought to life. Sometimes strength looks like trusting that God will not waste a hurt.

Sometimes strength simply looks like daring to say "even if not."

When you find yourself locked in the bathroom rocking away the hurts or with the covers pulled over your face mid-afternoon, hang on. When you're out and about, standing on solid ground, and still feel like you're drowning, look up. When no one sees you sinking down further and you feel alone in a crowd of people, He is there.

He calms the waves and settles the sea. We can call on the One who walks on water, knowing for certain that the waves that rock us must listen to His voice.

Don't give up, He's still writing. Light will break; the victory is already won. God's got this, whatever your "this" is, because God's got you. Even the bitter things can be sweet.

My worst nightmare came true and only years later would I realize that God used the broken spaces to prepare me for a medical road I never planned to walk. He taught me day in and day out to rely on Him for my next breath, for strength and hope and kindness, and in doing so He showed me that He would be more than enough for every situation. What was bitter was also sweet, even when I couldn't see past the moment.

And then from my worst nightmare came the miracle I could only dare to hope for. It took longer than I wanted, but it came right on time because God, He always knows best.

This is no longer just my story; it is our story, me and this best friend of mine. There will always be a piece of me that wishes we could go back in time and get the years back, but the bitter only makes the present even sweeter. She knows my past, I know hers, and there is a deep joy that comes in being able to say we can be fully known and yet still fully loved. We are learning again what "doing life together" means and although we have tasted the bitter, we are living the sweet.

It is an honor to attempt to put words to a miracle, knowing that this best friend of mine is cheering for every word and celebrating every sentence. We can't sign our names to this story, but trust me when I say that we are living testimonies that God doesn't waste a hurt. There is a purpose in the broken places.

He has broken but He has mended. He has torn but He has carried. And the truth of the matter is, when everyone ran out I wanted them back more than I wanted Him there. Just writing that makes me sick inside.

The road that I never wanted to travel, the journey that lasted years longer than I imagined, was ugly and dark and lonely and scary. It was bitter. It has left scars that may never fade.

My only companion on that road was Jesus and somewhere on that path, after many U-turns and roadblocks and thunderstorms of tears shed, I realized that the gift I wanted at the other side of my imagined rainbow was no longer friendships restored or hopes fulfilled — it was the One walking beside me. I only wanted Him and He was always mine to have.

He was the gift. He was what I wanted more than anything. Suddenly the darkness was lighter, the bitterness sweeter. I think something happens up in the heavenlies when we want God more than we want His promises. I think they dance.

When we let God do the mending, broken things can become blessed things. When I stumbled, God carried. When I wept, God loved deep. I wandered and God stayed. I wondered but God sang. He is the only story I have and the only one I want.

Luke 9:16 tells of Jesus feeding thousands with only five loaves of bread and two fish. But don't you know, He broke the bread and blessed it. And then that very bread became a blessing for thousands.

In Luke 24, just three days after Jesus was crucified, two of His disciples were walking along when a stranger "caught up" to them. They began to tell the stranger, who happened to be Jesus, of their sadness and confusion over Jesus' death. The Bible says they didn't recognize Him but after walking together for miles, they arrived at their destination and invited Him in for a meal. As they sat together at the table, Jesus took the bread, blessed it, and then broke it before giving it to them. In that moment, after the breaking and the blessing, their eyes were opened. They saw the glory sitting with them in their ordinary, the very glory that had been walking with them in their sadness. He was always there.

No one wants a story of brokenness, but it is often that very place of brokenness that Jesus gives thanks for and blesses as we say "even if not" while standing among dry bones.

As we walk in sadness or darkness or confusion and as we go about our ordinary, even there He breaks and blesses and keeps on showing up. I can't help but wonder what would happen if we gave thanks in those places, too.

Mine is an Ezekiel 37 story, one of dry bones and hope lost. But then God says "speak, prophesy to this dead place, proclaim healing and restoration and life. Believe the words I tell you to speak." The Word made flesh brought life to my dry bones and finally I could breathe. And with that very breath, I was hungry for Him.

Always, He is the best part of a story. Any story, every story. Look long enough and you'll see Him. You'll find Him in the broken places.

COMMUNITY
IS WORTH
fighting
FOR.

Chapter Four
loneliness & community

God can turn the thing that hurts you into the thing that heals you. He can take community-inflicted wounds and mature you, make you dependent on Him, and allow the body of Christ to play a big role in your healing. // Kristen Welch, Rhinestone Jesus

This morning I walked out of church after only one song.

Grabbing my bag, clutching my phone and hurrying to my car, I left without a second thought. It turns out you can walk out of church and still be going to church. It turns out there are people who can send one short text and you'll immediately drop everything for them.

And I know, you're either nodding your head because you have those people too, or you're shaking your head and longing to have both a church family and friends that are the church to you. I went a long time without both, and so I'm sitting here shaking my head, too.

I never saw this coming and I was prepared to live without it. For many years I was fully convinced love was a lie, a facade, and a joke. I was certain that every promise was only a disguised lie and everyone would leave. Community? It was dead to me. The church?

Well, the church with a capital C had burnt me, wounding me deeply. The people who said they loved Jesus, the ones who had been there through the thick and the thin, had all but disappeared. Overnight it was just me and Jesus.

Well, me and Jesus and a lot of lies shouting loud and sinking deep.

People talk about feeling alone and with just one word, whether you choose 'alone' or 'lonely,' I'm instantly transported back to that dark place. I'd like to tell you I've left it behind for the lighter spaces, but I find myself back on those familiar pathways again and again.

Sometimes you have to sit in the presence of Truth over and over, letting it wash over you, sinking deep inside and replacing the swirling lies. And you sit and sit some more because the lies, they can keep on coming even after you've been scrubbed clean.

I have people to pull me back and to lift me up when I've fallen, people who kneel in prayer when I'm all out of words. But can I be honest with you? It is such a struggle. I don't have this all figured out. Daily I'm faced with the choice of choosing love. Trusting in a quiet assurance of "I'll stay" when there are lies continuing to shout into the torn places is a fight. I've learned, though, that it is a battle worth entering into.

For years I would have told you without any hesitation that love was not worth the risk. Vulnerably opening back up and allowing someone to see the real me? Absolutely not, no thank you. Trusting again that people would come along and come around and love me for me, friends that wouldn't walk away when a hard time came? That didn't seem possible.

Life looked like showing up, facing the music, and trying to blend into the crowd. I was desperate for no one to see just how broken I was. But underneath that desperation I longed for someone, anyone, to look long and hard, see the broken places, and choose to sit in the mess with me. Have you ever tried to hide while praying for someone to come looking? Yeah, me too. Welcome to what we'll call the adult version of hide-and-seek.

Is everyone blind or am I actually this good at hiding the bruises, I wondered. *Does no one see me or do they see and not care,* I questioned.

I wanted to disappear just like those friendships had. Would anyone notice if I built walls and shut down? I wasn't sure and so I started building. But time had its way and all the while, without me even knowing it, God was having His way and He was building bridges.

There are many seasons of life and chapters of our stories that we could describe as bittersweet. Looking back, this is one of those times for me. In the moment, though, every day only felt bitter. But He is God and He is good, always healing the scars and bringing bones to life.

The blessing in the breaking is a gift that I have opened time and time again, over and over finding that I am more than okay with only Him. Community is worth fighting for but ultimately He is all we need.

And yet He *is* community and He is *for* community and so the walls needed to go. But no matter how hard I tried, how many hours and conversations and tears spent scratching the bricks and mortar, the walls remained. With every dent I made, I somehow laid yet another brick. It was a work only God could do.

Well, God and His people.

Much to my surprise, He brought them.

I longed for the Body of Christ to show Love to me, to see me in the crowd and choose to stick around. I was desperate for anyone to see the mess and be willing to grab their bag, hop in a car and come. I was willing to do those things for others and I pleaded for Him to bring people across my path who would love me in return.

But even if not, I had Him and I knew He would be enough. The loneliness was bearable because He kept on showing me I wasn't actually alone. But then God got a little funny, because sometimes He does that, and He used community to heal the wounds that community had left. He brought His people to me, lining them up along my path, taking the stones from the walls I built and laying them down to make a pathway straight in Him.

Sometimes I wish I knew when it all began to change inside but the truth is I think it was a slow turning, a gentle moving as He held me close, rocking me safely until reintroducing me to His Bride.

If community is a give-and-take thing, you may

feel that the emphasis seems to be on the taking. Maybe you've been burnt, your heart bruised black and blue, and you've chosen not to try again.

On the surface it makes sense. If community has wounded you, simply avoid community so you won't be wounded again, right? Well, not exactly.

I wish my heart knew this truth years ago, but by closing yourself off and pushing out any opportunity of love, you end up lonely and longing instead of seen and known. To the same extent that you allow yourself to feel sadness, you also allow yourself to feel joy. I didn't want the sadness and in closing myself off to the possibility of endings and hurts and betrayals, I also closed myself off to joy. I was scared and scarred and although lonely, I found myself resigned to the idea of "this is just how it will always be."

But God. Thank goodness, but God. I may have been resigned to that kind of life, but He wanted so much more for me.

He wants so much more for you.

Sometimes community plain hurts. Sometimes we'd much rather build walls than bridges. But I need you to force your eyes to read this slowly:

Jesus is enough. *Always.* But He is also Healer, Comforter, and all-knowing. He sees your hurts and your desire to be known and loved. Had you asked six years ago if the friendship that broke and brought the lies could heal and daily remind me of Truth, I would have said no. If you could sit down for coffee with the me from six years ago, she would emphatically tell you that it's easier to just do life alone. But she would have been so wrong. He created community. He *is* community. So hold onto Jesus and hold onto His promises. Your story isn't over.

There are people all around us who are hurting, people who are longing for community to see them and say they are welcome just as they are.

Can we be gut-level honest here? Too often we share what's happy and hide the hard. We'll settle for okay and fine — for ourselves and for one another. Because if you're fine, I'm fine. And if I'm fine, then don't you feel like you have to be, too? What a mess.

How on earth can we welcome one another in if our lives appear so perfect that others feel uncomfortable, so together that everyone else feels like a mess, so "I've been there, done that" while they're still finding their way through? It just doesn't work like that. We've got to meet them in the thick of it. We've got to show them our mess and sit with them in theirs.

Real Christ-honoring community welcomes the mess and calls it a masterpiece because it's a work-in-progress. Honest and beautiful community looks long and hard and says the story isn't over. It sits in the in between instead of hanging back and staying quiet until the sun is shining again.

Will you allow me to speak as the Church for a moment? Allow me to enter in and ask you to let us into the real? We want the smiles and the happy. Oh, how we want you to be overflowing, joy brimming all up to the top of your cup. But when the bad days come, and they will, don't cover up the hurting with the pleasant "I'm fine's." Don't skip over the hurts. Let's journey through them together. Let's share the broken places, the redeemed places, and the in-process spaces, too. We want to see them because when we do, we see *you*. Open the door, even just a crack. We're here.

I am absolutely, no doubt about it, imperfect. Easily annoyed and weak and a million other things, this book isn't written by someone who has it all together. I will never be that girl. I'm just the mess choosing to believe she is an in-process masterpiece. There are dark days and questions that still don't have answers. Even with people around me, there are lonely seasons.

A few months ago I found myself making a list of everything I needed, and I don't mean a grocery list or a to-do list, although I can make those like a boss. No, I was desperate to remember. In an attempt to quiet my soul and my mind, I ripped out a fresh page and began to list everything I wanted, everything that kept my mind spinning at night, everything I would have forked over big money for.

Answers.

Time.

Rest.

Happiness.

Open doors.

Love.

Encouragement.

More time.

Rest and answers and love. Time. And then more time because just a little bit wouldn't be enough. I stared at the list and the words written in ink. Slowly I began to drag the pen through each desperate cry, crossing each one off one at a time. And I can write about it and make it look nice but the truth is tears slipped down quietly but not so gracefully as I drew a long, dark line through those words.

And then I wrote *Jesus*. Only Jesus. Just Jesus.

Honestly, I don't want to be the girl with the happy face who has it all together. No, come look for the girl with puffy eyes holding up her tear-stained list. She may be messy and she sure won't have all the answers, but she'll tell you that all she wants is Jesus. She'll tell you that He will be enough because she has already tested that truth and found it to be solid and sure.

She might tell you to make a list, too. And if the word *friends* shows up on that list, you'll likely hear her reminding you that you already have one. His name is Jesus and He's not going anywhere.

When you aren't even looking because you've near given up hope, He brings His people to line the pathway leading you home. He sets the table and pulls out a chair, inviting you to get comfortable because there's no need to hold anything together. He holds the world and that means He holds you, too. He's got the loneliness covered. So put Him on the list. Then cross everything else off.

He'll be enough.

I received the email on April 16th. During my sixth semester of college, smack in the in between, I applied at the request of a friend and because it felt hypocritical not to, to be honest.

We call it God Stories. Once every semester, five or six students stand before their peers and tell a piece of their story. They do it to point to Jesus and to give God the glory. There is always a theme and for Spring 2014, we would be looking at renewal.

I had been before and listened to a few other students vulnerably open up and risk the battered, broken, mended parts of themselves. I teared up and left feeling inspired to keep on telling my own story.

Story is the word that has become a part of my being. I fall asleep thinking about stories, dream about them, and wake up to the next page. It's the word that creeps into everyday conversations so often that my friends just laugh or roll their eyes or make faces. They may think I don't notice, but the truth is I ignore it because I couldn't stop it if I tried.

I believe in the power of story and I believe we each have one, a story to be told. So when I read those words on April 16th, the email saying that yes, I had been chosen to stand in front of however many showed up, you might assume I smiled really big and felt excited.

But boy would you be completely wrong. Ask me

to meet you for a coffee date and I'm there. Invite me to share with your small group and I'm game. Tell me to hold a microphone and share my deepest wounds with a bunch of strangers and my clammy hands will shake as I lift them to your shoulders, begging you to tell me you're just kidding.

It wasn't a joke and the stage had never looked so intimidating, but I showed up and begged Him to show up in me.

I was flat out terrified but I called my people and just like Jesus, they showed up, too. One friend prayed over me before I entered the room, one introduced me to the sea of faces, and another filmed it so I could always remember that brave looks like saying yes to an April 16th email.

There wasn't a single moment I was alone, but not a single one of them could tell the story. There may be people walking the pages of your story with you, but only you can tell it.

You may not be given a microphone and you may never look out from a stage at faces of friends and strangers alike, but every day you show up to life you can show up ready to tell your story, to hold it in your hands like an offering ready to be poured out.

I don't know who was in that room. There are dozens of people who know some of the most intimate details of my story and I don't even know their names. But because I trust the One who wrote the pages and is authoring my life into a best seller, just like every other story He writes, I sat down on the edge of the stage and got eye-level and gut-honest with the messy and the redeemed. The thing about renewal is that for something to be renewed, there are going to be ugly, messy valleys of dead bones to wade through. It isn't pretty.

But when you feel Him calming your racing heart and you look out and find your community sitting there encouraging you on, even as you share the lies you're still battling, you can pour the broken out as an offering, thanking Him for every set of ears hearing your mess because it tells only of His glory.

There's a quote by Corrie ten Boom that hung above my bed for years. She said, "Every experience God gives us, every person He puts in our lives, is the perfect preparation for the future that only He can see."

Sounds about right.

However, wouldn't it be really handy and convenient — although perhaps also obnoxious — if some sort of siren went off inside alerting you each time you've met one of your people? Instead, at least for me, He brings them all quiet-like, slowly slipping my people in, writing them into the story in ways I couldn't have seen coming.

As I type this I'm sitting at a long wooden table in a bustling coffee shop. There's chatter in the background and the smell of roasted coffee beans fills the air. It's one of my favorite places in Birmingham, partly for the coffee but mainly for the community.

I've been staring at the blinking cursor, trying to figure out what I could possibly write without awk-

wardly crying and making my table-sharing neigh-
bors uncomfortable.

Catch me at the right time and the word *Birmingham* will make me cry. I can't even help it, I just love
this place so much. The city is a beautiful mix of old
and new. It gives a big southern welcome no matter
where you go, the sky displays the most beautiful
sunsets I've ever seen, and everything about it feels
like home.

When I came here for college, I moved twelve
hours away from the place and the people I knew
best. I came to a city where no one knew my name
and truthfully, I liked it that way. It was a fresh start,
a new beginning. But somewhere in those four years
Birmingham became more than the address I wrote
in the upper-left corner of an envelope.

Birmingham is where my people are. These
strangers-turned-friends that entered into the story
are home to me. It's not really about this place; it's
about the people.

They have walked my road with me, journeyed
through the darkness and held my hand until I could
see the light, shown me Jesus in their words and actions, and made me laugh until I fell to the floor.
They have been a safe place for secret sharing, the
first people I tell exciting news, and my late night
drive companions. These people have seen me dance
and have joined in. They've put up with my not-so-
lovely singing in the car. We have inside jokes and
memories that will last a lifetime. We've road tripped
and left the country on mission trips and gone on
milkshake runs when we should have been fast
asleep. These are the people that will watch Netflix

with me for hours on end, whisper jokes in class so we'll both stay awake, put up with my need to take a picture of basically everything, and listen to me ramble as I tell stories over a shared meal.

They have carried me to the feet of Jesus more times than I can count. They have held my heart securely, prayed for me intently, and loved me fiercely.

And so as I sit on this wooden bench typing away, tears sting my eyes. He was enough and would have been enough even if He didn't bring His people to me. Yet I sit here with tears in my eyes because the girl so broken by community has fallen head over heels in love with it once again.

So many of my richest moments are with them, sacred moments when I have felt the Father's love by the way that we love each other. We've walked messy roads that have broken us, but we have rebuilt. We have misunderstood and made it right, we've loved until it hurt and then loved some more, we have invited and pulled up another seat, always another seat, because there is always more grace and more room. Even when we show up empty handed, we come for one another, leaving wherever we are to be with our people and to love them hard. These people have shown up to celebrate the joys and they have held me in the sad times. They are a part of my story and really, we're all just walking each other home.

You know that overused phrase "doing life together"? Well, we're doing that.

In her memoir about friendship, Melanie Shankle wrote, "That's how you know your true friends: you hear their laughter and look into their eyes, and it feels like coming home."[1]

They are home to me.

The tattered tapestry has been re-woven and sometimes my life feels like one big quilt with a whole lot of patches and sewn up stitches.

I'm running this race bound for the finish line with that quilt tied around me like a cape, and all I want is to hear "well done my good and faithful servant."

But now it's different because I'm no longer running silently through the crowd or running away from the crowd; I'm running my own race with a crowd of witnesses cheering me on. I have found community and love again. It's still messy. It is such hard work. Some days continuing to show up feels like more of a struggle than a joy. But here's the truth: community is worth fighting for. God Himself is three-in-one. He is so for community and so we must be, too.

Someone said it to me once, way back in middle school. There are one thousand things I've blocked out from those days but of all the advice I've heard since then, I've never lost these words: People and relationships are like elevators. They will either take you up or they will take you down but they will never leave you the same.

We can all keep building up walls and breaking down behind them, but what if we chose to risk one more time, reach out one more time, take that one tiny but brave step that feels so big and absolutely gut-wrenchingly raw? What if we chose to stretch our hands out, only to find them slipped into the hand of another? What if we looked up into their eyes and it felt like coming home?

It likely won't happen all at once. Beauty comes out of the ashes and sometimes we have to march around the walls we've built seven times, seven conversations, seven brave steps or seven years of prayers until they start falling down. But oh, friend, keep on marching. Because when those walls tumble and crumble down, you may find that while you've been marching your sisters were peering over, heard your cries for community, and took up their own sledgehammers and notecards and coffee dates and they've been trying to get through. Community is coming for you.

you become what you behold

Chapter Five

small & seen

You become like what you behold.[1]

A lot of road was walked in between the broken places and the community of now.

To be clear, the woman writing these words today still holds the broken little girl of yesterday. She is both, yesterday and today walking into tomorrow. Walking and stumbling, she picked up lies, calling them truths while sticking them in her back pocket for the road ahead.

Sometimes the little girl in me turns them over and over, feeling lies that are rough like rocks, cutting and bruising myself as they fall out and land hard. Other times I reach in and my calloused hands pull out a smooth stone, weathered flat from the many times I've rubbed it in between my fingers. Lies can sound like truths if you aren't careful. The smooth stones are deceiving, worn from much too much time carrying the lies in my hands.

After enough time, the extra weight you've picked up simply becomes a part of your being. You can't remember a time without the bulging pockets. Was there really a time when you enjoyed the journey and kept your eyes ahead or have you always walked with eyes down, bending over time and again to reach for the pebbles under your feet? Didn't you walk right over the lies in times past? Wasn't there a time that, with eyes straight forward, you reached for the Truth that pulls you to bow instead of bend? Have your hands always been cut and torn from holding rocks slowly worn into smooth stones?

I bought a lot of lies; I bent for too many rocks. Desperate to be fully known and yet fully loved, I searched for my significance in the eyes of others and placed my worth in their hands, even while trusting that the most important thing about me was Jesus. I was a walking contradiction, finding my value in Him but pleading for others to validate that value.

Love itself seemed like a lie while at the very same time it became an idol.

I wanted to be seen as a good friend, as kind and compassionate and encouraging, strong and capable. I knew I was a daughter of God but I thought I needed someone else to see it and say so, too. I felt inconsequential, insignificant, invisible. The louder the lies, the heavier the pockets, the smaller I became.

We were never meant to compare and contrast our lives with others and as long as we continue to measure our success or goodness or worth against another, we will never see clearly.

At one of her speaking engagements, Shauna Niequist so clearly stated, "With people, you can either connect or compare but you can't do both."

But there I was, reaching for a love that would never satisfy. I wanted man's applause so much that I missed the fact that I already had God's approval. Let's be honest, it's still a daily struggle, a constant re-humbling.

When my people walked away, I felt both small and unseen. I put the two feelings together, hating the brokenness they brought, never realizing that one could be good and one wasn't true in the first place. Small scared me because in my mind it equaled being invisible. If I was small, no one would see me. If no one saw me, no one would know me and love me.

The people-pleaser in me went full-throttle, foot to the ground. It didn't look any different than before because I was always the "good girl." My version of rebelling looked like watching Gilmore Girls in the afternoon, even though I wasn't allowed to. If you're looking to trade rebellious stories, I'm not your girl.

In two different plays I was handed the script of the "good Christian." My friends jokingly call me Mom and I respond without a second thought. I'm a Type-A firstborn, an ISFJ according to Myers-Briggs, and I really want you to like me. It didn't take long before the goody-two-shoes roles and the quick comments that reflected the pedestal I was placed on in the eyes of others began to feel like a noose around my neck. I listened to the lies whispering in the dark that everyone was waiting for me to fail, to fall. The platform called Reputation felt shaky, always just one step away from crumbling. When the brokenness came and loneliness followed right behind, what I had believed to be true crumbled around me and so I picked up the rocks and began to build.

I built an impressive resume. I went on mission trips and built houses. I added more and more to my plate and none of it was bad. Please know, my heart was in it for the right reasons. But deep inside I hoped that these good things, these somewhat impressive acts, would be for His glory, yes, but would also earn just a little bit of your affection and attention.

Ann Voskamp says this about that particular type of building and reaching, "When you are wrung out, that is the sign you've been reaching for rungs."[2]

My plate was full, my resume long but my soul dry. Rest was a foreign concept and small didn't seem like a very good thing to be.

But then I went to Haiti.

Somewhere in between bending down for lies that told me bigger was better and hopping on a plane for a foreign country, I started to see my smallness as a gift.

I have wrestled with this chapter for weeks, my mind spinning wildly through one million moments in time, attempting to figure out when I began to see my own size as a grace gift. But I'm here, right here, weeks later with the only answer being that those one million small moments were teaching me my own smallness, teaching me to say "even if not" all over again, believing that He would still be so very good even if the only one who ever knows my name is the One who made me.

Nothing happened overnight, but as I look back I see moments no one thought much of, times community came around me, noticed the stones I kept turning over, and began to speak Truth to me instead. I remember that it sounded ludicrous at first, but they just kept showing up and speaking truth. They took the weights I had carried from my hands and they carried me to Jesus.

Small started to become the most uncomfortable comfortable. When held up against who God is, I am minuscule. Yet He knows how many hairs are on my head, and this is no small feat because I lose at least thirty-five every time I brush my hair.

He shows me I am small and known all at once. I've picked up that truth and I carry it with me like a feather, light and breezy and practically weightless.

It took several sets of three hundred and sixty-five for me to glimpse the truth that nothing I do or don't do can add or take away from the love He has for me. The broken is becoming the mended, the lonely girl inside now walks with friends who love her like family. My pockets are a bit lighter. And yet this 'even if not,' the one that calls me to leave the platform building and resume boosting, the 'even if not' that says I'll trust Him even if I'm only seen by Him, it is my daily hard.

But then I stand under the great expanse of Haitian sky and all is righted, all back in its place, and I can distinctly feel my own smallness. My smallness is a shocking relief, a comfort, and there isn't time to be taken aback by the balm small is to my soul as I stare into the dark of night. It is unusual and weird and settled inside it feels so right. Whether blue sky or white expanse or the moon shining so bright, my eyes are finally fixed upward instead of on myself. Suddenly the weight of my smallness feels light, my pockets empty of rocks.

Why do I forget to pick this feeling up and place it inside? Or, perhaps, why do I miss the truth of it carried inside my soul? I forget to look up. I forget to remember. My eyes are busy looking and my hands distractedly reaching for a place in this world, but then I look at the sky and I remember as the broken places re-member all over again.

Smallness is a present, not a punishment.

This particular time the velvet black sky held more light than my eyes were accustomed to seeing. It's a weird feeling to look around at eye level and see darkness, only to look up and see the sky aglow. Back home, city lights and street lamps and a world of quick stops and fast food light up around us but they are only a distraction from the Light.

We didn't travel to Haiti to see the sky light up, but there we were and there it was. Go where it's real dark, no earthly lights to distract you, and then raise your head to the sky.

If I had to guess, you'll want to raise your hands, too.

We stood there, silently gathered beneath the blanket of bright lights, thinking and praying, humming worship songs quietly. One by one as we were ready, we walked back inside and gathered around the long table.

Gathered under the majesty. Gathered around the table. And there was God, present in both.

Read aloud over our team were the words of Philippians 2:14-16: Do everything without grumbling or arguing, so that you may become blameless and pure, children of God without fault in a warped and crooked generation. Then you will shine among them like stars in the sky as you hold firmly to the word of life.

The sentence about the stars came to a close, short and sweet, and then it was my turn to speak, to offer encouragement to those around me. I had been thinking all day long about what I would say, practicing in my head words that could come out and strengthen, reach out and encourage, but when I found comfort in my own smallness there wasn't anything left to offer but Jesus.

I sat there and my mouth moved and He spilled out these words: You don't have to be cut out. Because of Christ, you've already been placed in. We don't have to be more or try harder to achieve worldly success; we just have to shine like the stars against the dark of night.

It sounds a little bit cheesy but I've found it to be true: we are all small but together we shine. Standing quietly underneath the sky, I returned once again to my own smallness; humbled on the cracked pavement, reminded of who He is and who I am in comparison. And yet the gentle whisper of wind blowing through the trees reminded me that who I am has changed because I am found in Him.

He is my identity, my safe place, my fortress in the

storm and comfort in the dark of night. He is vast and large and loud. His hands formed my hands and He calls me to lay down the rocks and pick up my cross.

The God who takes the time to name each star says that I shine. I huff and puff as I journey the rough terrain and He breathes out stars because apparently that's no big deal. So if His breath comes out as stars and yet He says that I am to shine in my generation like the stars in the sky, I'm going to just take Him at His word. When it comes to shining, He seems to know what He's talking about.

For me, this looks like laying down rocks and carrying the Light. Today this looks like taking the smooth stones of lies held too long and placing them at His feet, an altar unto Him.

He keeps teaching me this lesson because I keep on forgetting. I rush and hustle and hurry and build all the wrong things, stand when I should sit down and stay silent when I should speak up. I get loud when He whispers quiet, *"Hey, you know I've got this, right?"* I listen to the lies and forget the Truth has been walking with me every step of the way.

Maybe it's just me, but I can become so focused on being enough or concerned with wanting to be seen as a bunch of good things that I convince myself to do more of something, less of another thing, and just be better. At what, I'm not always sure. But always, better.

I get small, feel thin, hear the lies, forget the truth, long to be seen, stand up and get a little bit loud but then His Word gets louder and I get small and here we go again.

But there's one truth I've picked up and continue to turn over. I'm carrying this one in my heart, that Christ is more than enough and Christ is in me, and so therefore the striving can cease.[3]

There are all these thin places that speak of His grace, calloused spaces that tell the struggle. I see fingerprints of His goodness all over my life but He keeps on handing me opportunities to get small and smaller still and tell Him yet another "even if not."

Honestly, sometimes I'd just rather not. Sometimes I think it would be easier to go along with the crowd. Sometimes small feels like a real bad idea. We were made to cheer and champion, not compare and compete, and yet my human nature continues to forget.

But then I stand under the dark of night and am swallowed whole by His presence. I open my hands and drop the rocks. The breeze blowing through the trees seems to whisper that I can either carry my frustrations and worries about the unknown or choose to be still and be known. The sky stays dark and silent but I hear it clear as day: I can run myself ragged until my soul is weary or I can slow down and take the time to listen to listen instead of listening to respond. I can get smaller still.

Without the hustle and bustle, I hush and stare at stars that are always there but seem to disappear in the bright lights of the culture I'm so used to where bigger is better and small feels silly. But here I am, small yet seen. Fully known under the cover of a dark night, yet fully loved.

He calls the stars by name and He calls me to shine just as bright. My soul is at home in the small and I promise I don't even realize I'm praying it until it's over, the words tumbling inside and landing right where they belong:

Breather of stars, may I remember to dream big and stay small. May I always find my place at Your feet and not in rung climbing or stats or followers. There is only One worth following and it's You. I've had enough of platforms. I think I'll build altars instead.

I have a thing for Tuesdays. If I had to marry a day of the week, that would totally be the one. In its unobtrusive spirit, Tuesday invites me to breathe again and relish the normal of an ordinary day. Sunday is Sabbath and I love it dearly. But then Monday comes and takes our breath away with all of its to-do lists and planning and well, all the things. Wednesday is that uncomfortable middle when we're wishing the rest of the days would just hurry up for the weekend's arrival.

Tuesday is grace.

It is a fresh look at normal life after Monday has rushed as all around. Tuesday is when I begin to breathe again. Tuesday reminds me to slow down, to get small, and to make room for Christ to be so very big. He already is and my recognizing His greatness won't make Him any greater, but it does change how I view myself and my life in light of who He is.

My friend Emily Freeman loves Tuesday, too. Many of her words have brought me back to my own smallness, and for that I will always be grateful. Every Tuesday, she encourages her online friends to stop, hit the pause button, and look for the beauty of the ordinary because moments don't hold meaning themselves, but meaning is found when we recognize the presence of Christ with us in those moments.

In her book *Simply Tuesday*, Emily says, "Jesus came to earth to extend a personal invitation for us to enter into his kingdom rather than try to build our own...I'm exploring what it looks like to release my obsession with building a life and embrace the life Christ is building in me."[4]

It seems opposite of our culture and this generation, really. It goes against the grain to sit for a bit in the quiet, to listen to our questions, to let love be the loudest message of our lives. But our souls weren't made for platforms and our hands weren't meant to build a stage — we're called to build altars.

I've found that when I move my eyes from His Word to the paths others are walking, my feet — and my heart, and my thoughts, and my actions — tend to follow. I start looking to the left or the right and I forget to run my own race. I stop for a drink on the sidelines and end up becoming a watcher, not a runner. I compare and contrast and get so focused on how fast her legs are pumping or how much distance she's covered that my legs stop moving and my run turns to a crawl. When my eyes turn from Him to them, I can't help but slow my pace to observe theirs. I get small, real small, when I compare my ways to hers, my stats to theirs, my dreams to their realities.

After years of struggling to be okay with my own

smallness, I find myself there. I am small and I feel it, but it is for all the wrong reasons. Obsessed with those around me, I focus on a race I was never meant to run.

The irony is not lost on me, how for years I struggled to be okay with being small in their eyes and seen by His, yet when I find my smallness with them instead of Him, I miss the entire point.

As I sat in an open-walled Haitian church on a Sunday morning this past March, He brought me back to the right kind of small. Every day my soul fights to remain in that space.

I know that I'm writing these words to you from my kitchen table in Birmingham, but if I close my eyes I swear I'm there, my head slightly bent to the right, my ears straining to catch every third word translated into English. It was church and it was beautiful, even when I didn't understand what was being said. There were a couple lines that I did make out, though, and as I quickly tapped them into the notes section of my phone, I knew they were already leaving an imprint on my heart:

Stay in your lane. Watch and see God take care of everything. Love His things more than worldly things. Help others but to the glory of God. Choose Jesus over everything else. Lift Him higher, higher. Fix your eyes on Him.

Fix your eyes, build an altar instead of a platform, and run your race.

Jen Hatmaker, in her honest, blunt, encouraging way, has said it like this, "Do your thing. Play your note. We are all watching and learning, moved. You are making the world kinder, more beautiful, wiser, funnier, richer, better...Run your race."[5]

There's a difference between playing small and getting small. One says your gifts are illegitimate and the other says the gifts you've been given are all from Him.

We've got a message to share because we simply must be the generation that says every story matters no matter what chapter we're in. We have to be the ones who will say "even if not." We are living in the ampersand of small and seen and listen, we've got to say that we have met Jesus here, too. We absolutely must be most concerned with spreading the message of His truth and love because grace doesn't discriminate, it moves. So I get small all over again. I pull the rocks from my pockets and build an altar. I look down at my feet standing on the sideline, tighten the laces, and get back in the race.

I don't want the platform, not really. Our souls weren't made for a stage, but neither were we made to play small. Instead, God's love and glory is displayed in brilliance and greatness in and through our smallness. Small is not the same as shrinking back and this "even if not" looks a little bit different than the rest. Even if I am never handed a microphone or an actual book deal, even if I'm remembered only by a handful, living in the in between of big and small still finds me seen and known. I don't need to play small, I simply get small.

In her book *Make it Happen*, Lara Casey wrote about living out of her smallness. "Your playing small does not serve the world," she said. "You never know how long you have left here on this earth to love others and change them for the better in that love. Taking bold action on what matters starts a powerful domino effect. The good you do today changes generations. Life is too short and too vulnerable to coast through, living by accident."[6]

The world will keep moving fast and faster and we'll never truly be able to keep up. But honestly, we were never meant to. We've got one race to run. I've got mine and you've got yours and they'll both take us home but the journey will look different. Lap after lap, "even if not" after "even if not," we get small and make room for Him to show up real big.

The small moments can seem unnoticed, unheard of, unseen. Or maybe they're none of these things, but they just happen to often get pushed aside. Big moments can get a lot of hype and it's often well deserved. That doesn't mean small is any less important, though.

Just a few weeks after moving into my first apartment I was standing over the kitchen sink, slowly and methodically rinsing and slicing strawberries, when I caught myself thinking, "I really enjoy this."

Quiet. Easy. So simple. Not a big deal and certainly not life changing. But the thought caught me and held on for a bit, likely because it falls right in line with what I've spent the past several months learning and re-learning: the spiritual practice of finding and choosing quiet causes something in our souls to twist up tight and then unwind with relief.

We do one thing while thinking about or preparing for the next. Our thumbs scroll lit up iPhone screens while we stand in line at the checkout counter. We enter into June with relief but there's a part of us already thinking ahead to starting back up in August. We are present, but we are not. We do, do, do so we can be, be, be but I can't figure out just what we're all trying to be.

It was some time back in February or March that I stopped listening to music in the car. My phone was always dinging, there was always someone to talk to, homework or words to intake and a checklist to finish. I was just a few months away from graduating college and according to the questions I received each day, I was supposed to have my life figured out by that point.

There was so much noise and my soul was begging for quiet.

So I turned the dial off. Not down, but *off*. I don't even know where I was headed but I do remember the odd, almost awkward minutes of silence. I wanted to fill them with something. A phone call, text message alert, country songs, talk radio, anything.

But I sat there in the silence and quickly the twisting inside turned to sweet relief. I didn't know how much my soul was craving a moment of silence until the noise disappeared.

I kept the radio off in my car for months and began to look for other ways to quiet my life. I said no more often. I gracefully bowed out of a few opportunities. I skipped things I never would have missed. I didn't show up to stand on a stage and receive an important honor at a ceremony because I was sitting in the quiet of my room writing out a homework assignment.

I was still working, still doing, but there was a slow shift inside as I began to live out the truth that people are more important than platforms and relationships matter more than results. I purposely chose the semi-dark of a room lit with white Christmas lights and a computer screen over an award, a stage, clapping and fluorescent lighting. And I breathed easier because of it.

Yes, there is a time and place for the noise. Believe me, I attended many things with a whole lot of noise. I didn't stop my life, I simply started to recognize a pull toward the quieter places.

I thought a lot more. I felt a bit deeper. I wrestled with some tough stuff. The quiet made room to hear Him speak.

Months later I found myself standing over a colander full of just-washed strawberries, thinking how lovely and enjoyable the moment was.

Not for Instagram or a viral blog post, but for my soul. It was beautiful for my soul. I've washed and rinsed countless strawberries since that early summer afternoon. Without fail, as one hand gently holds each berry and the other cuts the fruit, juice runs over my fingers as I think how simple and sweet the little things can be.

I'm learning to savor the small and to choose the unhurried path. I'm still running my race, but this lap seems to be one of quiet, of bowing in worship instead of bending for rocks, of standing under a dark stretch of sky and raising my eyes because though I am small, I am known. Small tastes like strawberries and freedom.

god's
LOVE STORY
spans the
GLOBE

Chapter Six
here & there

It's a funny thing coming home. Nothing changes. Everything looks the same, feels the same, even smells the same. You realize what's changed is you. // F. Scott Fitzgerald

There is literally no explanation for it. Unlike any behavior that falls in line with who I tend to be, I signed up, said yes, paid money and got on a plane.

I had done all those things before, certainly, but always with enough heads up to wrap my mind around every possible detail. But this time I didn't know the people, the place, or the plan once we arrived. This time I had nothing to do with it all. This time God was taking me to Haiti.

I will never be the same.

I've become a walking version of the song that never stops playing. Have you ever been startled to find yourself humming a tune or dancing to a song in your head that you didn't even realize you were singing? And then you stand there in complete confusion, desperately trying to figure out where it came from and how it got there? Have you ever traced your steps back far enough to realize you heard the song on the radio three days earlier and, apparently, it got stuck somewhere inside and has been on repeat ever since?

That is me and Haiti is the track that never stops. She shows up in casual conversations and deep discussions, in my dreams and in my waking moments, in blog posts and movies and I kid you not, a girl just walked by me as I write these words at the library, and what did she say? "Maybe I can find a book here about Haiti."

Haiti is stuck on repeat in my life.

No one told me I was signing up to be wrecked by God. No one, least of all me, saw it coming. I had been to several other places; I had seen poverty and sunken cheekbones, ribs nearly exposed and houses made out of sun-weathered blue tarps.

But I had not been to Haiti. I don't know just how it works, but I can't help but wonder if God purposely planted part of my heart in the Haitian dirt when He formed me. All this time I was walking around thinking I was a whole person, but then I went there and felt a piece of myself I hadn't known come fully alive. First, though, I would have to feel the breaking.

I am there.

Everywhere you turn there is another lesson to be learned, another story to listen to, a child to push on a rusted swing set and a set of hands outstretched, waiting silent and patient for a bowl of rice and beans.

Streets as we know them in America do not exist.

Everyone is going and moving in all directions, animals crossing the road at any given time, noises blaring and smells wafting and all of it, all at one time, everywhere. Bright colors stand in stark contrast to the mud brown houses and pathways and skin and eyes. They walk with dignity like you've never seen and when they smile, something lights up inside of you at the mere sight. There is unimaginable beauty and undeniable poverty no matter where your eyes land, but in the despair and the dirt there is more hope and joy than humanly possible.

This is Haiti, the land of the forever hallelujah, the place where joy and sorrow meet and mingle until you can't see one without the other. There is darkness darker than you've ever seen. There is light brighter than you've ever imagined.

In so many ways, Haiti is my ampersand, my in between. When I am here, in a place with clean, running water and a Starbucks on every other corner, a part of me wants to be there. When I am there, first-world worries fade away and my biggest concern becomes how I can best encourage the broken sets of eyes that belong to the little hands that slip into mine, and yet when I'm gut-level honest I long for air conditioning and iced coffee and maybe I also miss Instagram.

As soon as I breathed the Haitian air on a Friday afternoon in 2014, I became a walking ampersand, the real life version of these words: You will never be completely at home again because part of your heart will always be elsewhere. That is the price you pay for the richness of loving and knowing people in more than one place.

This "even if not" feels like a combination of all the others, each moment and lesson and season wound up into one.

I question why I was born in America and why they were born in Haiti. I wonder why He doesn't seem to step in and save the day.

I look into the eyes of a little boy who is likely a teenager with bones that didn't grow big and tall because he has never known a full meal, and I wince as I hear that he walked for three hours just to receive Tylenol at the once-a-week clinic.

I hold tightly to the little brown hands that slip into mine as we walk down the winding pathways and I can't help but feel the cracked skin as it rubs against mine. We walk past houses that we would never dare to deem houses in America, and after the first two or three I am no longer struck by the broken cracks in the dried mud because in Haiti that is just the norm. Skin and mud houses and everywhere, you'll find brokenness if you look for it.

And there I am, pale white skin and thick brown hair. I stand out and don't belong and although I am home in a way I never expected, there is a deep loneliness and an ache inside. I am smaller than I knew possible, so small I can't possibly be found, but He finds me there and flips the coin, turns everything over and writes an ampersand into the story, promising that there are more pages to come. He is the Answer I'm looking for and the only thing they actually need, more than water or medicine or peanut butter crackers. He is healing and mending hurts that I can't see on the outside. There is joy deeper than I've ever known and at any given moment dancing is likely to break out as little bones and old bones alike move to an unheard song.

Haiti is my ampersand, the culmination of so many of my "even it not's" and the place that asks me to lay them at His feet. Sure, He could choose to save the day in the way I imagine it in my head. But the truth is that He'll be just as good if He instead asks me to daily say, "Yes, Lord, I'll love You even if not."

He knew it would happen this way, how I'd board a plane and never come back the same. As He so often does in my life, God gave me one word to cling to while I was there. He placed the word *open* on my heart and there I was, fully convinced that He had called me to go and openly share my story to bring Him glory.

But I was so very wrong in believing that would be the end of it. Open? Yes. Open to the quiet, to being still, to listening and mulling over. Open to silence and questions and doubts. Open to wrestling and turning over and open to looking hard at the darkness and searching for the light. Open to returning and waiting and sitting until He gave the go ahead to speak.

I thought I was going with the purpose of talking about Jesus, but He took me there to break me, to split me wide open and open wide my eyes and ears and heart to His ways, to bring me to a place where I could never deny what I had seen and would forever have to daily choose to whisper the words, whether I'm here or there, that I'll love Him even if not.

The purples of my eyelids become the brown dirt roads and hills barren of trees. The bright white smiles against dark skin shine bright and when I open my eyes I'm back in a place where it's comfortable to be comfortable. I'm here, not there, right in this middle ground and still caught between the two.

I was a closed book for weeks, returning empty and quiet. I had sat and soaked in the stories but I didn't know what to say or how to say anything at all.

Everything felt like a mess and suddenly it seemed as if I didn't belong anywhere, part of my heart within me and another piece one thousand miles away.

It had been everything I was expecting and nothing like I thought it would be. Wrestling with that in a land of air conditioning and more comforts than I know what to do with was culture shock in a whole new way. But *open* had a purpose beyond Haiti and so I slowly began to discover what the word would mean here, not there.

Eventually it all came spilling and seeping and pouring out with a force so strong it was almost violent. As soon as the book was opened, the stories came so fast and furious that I could barely keep up with myself. It felt a little bit like a free-fall but then there was Jesus, catching me in a downward spiral of tears and stories and sights and sounds and smells.

Every day I carry Haiti with me. I take a breath and walk out the door and if we ever meet one day, you won't know it right away but you will have just encountered a piece of Haiti, no passport required.

Heaven come to earth. It's a phrase I've heard thrown around here and there without too much thought, but then I found myself crying in the middle of I-don't-know-where and in that moment, I got it.

We were all sharing two benches, our team opening up packages of peanut butter crackers and passing them around as the men of the village began to join us. They smiled and sat down, silent. Our benches made a V shape and a circle was created as they filled in across from us.

It was unintentional, I'm sure, but God knew and I think He was smiling.

It's strange to think how oddly normal it all seemed in that moment, licking peanut butter off my lips, offering crackers to the men who joined us and smiling at the children shyly hiding behind the weathered tree.

They looked at us; we looked at them. We didn't share a language and the words unspoken were almost palpable — how do we build a bridge?

We asked a few questions and one or two men would look at the others and then answer for the group. We watched their faces and listened intently as they thanked us for coming. And then it happened — men began to speak up and say they had prayed for years and watched nearby villages receive help but nothing changed in their own corner of the world. They looked at us and dared to speak the truth of what life had looked like for so long. "We thought God had forgotten us," they said. "We asked Him what we had done wrong and why no one would come for us."

My eyes filled with tears as I forced myself to blink fast and look hard into their worn faces. No one turned away. We were strangers sitting under the wide open sky learning how to relate to one another, and then they shared their brokenness with us and I was undone.

Forgotten by God? It took us hours just to reach the clearing; how would anyone have stumbled upon this village? But where had I been and what was so important that I hadn't come sooner? Blinking fast wasn't helping and the longer I looked into their broken places the more I began to see my own brokenness.

But then they kept speaking because, of course, there was an ampersand. The story wasn't over.

With my eyes still brimming, one man shared that when our organization provided money for a well that would provide clean water, something they had never known, it was like heaven coming down to earth.

He said it just like that. *Heaven coming down to earth.*

And He was right, but it wasn't us that brought heaven down. No, it was that moment right there, arm touching arm and story intertwining with story. That's what it's supposed to look like. Different colors, different languages, one same God.

With hope in their eyes and confidence in their voices they asked permission to pray over us. Lowering my face into my hands, desperate to not make them feel uncomfortable but unable to do anything but weep, I listened as they thanked God that we came and praised Him for Christ in us.

Sometimes heaven looks like a circle of strangers with nothing in common except the One thing that matters most.

I am here.

In the left turn lane at the corner of Wildwood and Lakeshore, I stare out the window and hum the melody, singing the refrain under my breath.

It's another typical, ordinary day of the mundane and the strain of "returning to normal" is picking at me. Sometimes I find myself beginning to think something is wrong with me because I can't seem to pack it all up and return to what was and what used to be before I stepped on Haitian soil. But if pieces of your heart are left behind then how in this big wide world can it all be put back together again?

I stare out the window, oblivious to the words on the radio and the sound escaping my lips, thinking of to-do lists and letters to write, what I need to pick up at the store and oh yes, I should call my grandparents.

I sing the refrain in the middle of all the mundane and within seconds my glazed over eyes are dripping with tears instead of visualizing the layout of the grocery store. I no longer hear the radio singing the tune; suddenly it's just me, a crinkled sheet of paper filled with printed words, and the expanse of Haitian blue sky.

I'm back under the roof of the open-walled church. I hear Kristie, one of the missionaries we're staying with, leading the teenagers around us. We sit on eight benches crammed with people hanging off the edges. A square of song, they've come to practice for the Easter service. They think we've come to help them practice singing in English, but we've just come to love them.

On a Sunday afternoon with rainclouds rolling in the distance, that is exactly what we sit down to do. We're all mixed up, pale arm touching dark skin as they hold tight to the words before them and raise their voices, soft at first, to sing. We've come to help but first we must listen.

The first line escapes and I know the tune by heart. There's a catch in my throat as I look around at the beautiful brown faces of brothers and sisters I have never met, singing together the words to *Lord, I Need You.*[1]

By the chorus Kristie reminds us to jump in and sing. After all, we're sitting close enough that every personal bubble is being popped in twenty directions, all so they can hear how we pronounce the words and copy the movement of our mouths. I open my lips and mutter the words, struck by the power of a Sunday afternoon song in the mountains of Haiti, until I remember I should sing out so they can hear.

I don't normally do that. When the house is empty, I run my hands along the black and white keys and belt out whatever tune comes to mind. When I'm alone, I spin in the living room and dance in the dorm room and sing loudly in the car. But this is not the time to be shy and so the whisper turns into singing as mourning turns into dancing and I look at the faces, each of the faces, and I realize they mean the words they're saying.

I must have uttered the refrain one hundred times but this time it's different. My voice swells and I wonder if it's too loud, but the boy to my right sings louder and I realize the freedom I have found has given him the freedom to learn, to listen and to sing with confidence in a language he barely knows.

A few more times through and they switch to creole, taking their eyes off the papers and singing the words their hearts already know.

He nods his head, inching the crinkled paper in my direction. His arm scratches against mine and I take in the words, all jumbled up into something I don't recognize, and I sound them out all awkward and sing-song like.

My smile is wide and I sing the words in creole that I would believe in any language. The boy to my right, more man than boy, really, smiles and I know I must sound funny. I sing it louder, all these messed up pronunciations, and at the end he turns to me and says I did a good job. Somewhere inside I know those words are from my Father.

I stare up at the never-ending blue sky and blink fast until I realize I'm looking at Alabama sky and Haiti once again feels a world away. Tears are choking my throat and the ugly cry is threatening, but I stumble through the words anyway. I re-member the pieces by remembering and it all comes together, the memories and the sound of my voice, the tears sliding down my cheeks as the stoplight turns green.

Pulling myself together, I go about my Americanized way of shopping and buying and purchasing anything and everything on my list. I load the car and as I exit the parking lot I see a man with a megaphone. I drive past his signs as I hear the shouting mumblings of confusion, all mixed up in what goes into the megaphone and out of the speakers.

Honk if you love Jesus. Pull over if you don't want to go to hell. Jesus loves you.

I sigh and wonder if it does any good. Do people ever pull over? Does it turn more people off than it invites in?

Do I?

Lord I need You, oh I need You. In the mountains of Haiti and on the streets of Birmingham, I need You. My hope, my light, will You help me see? Oh Lord, don't let go of me.

My heart rewrites the words and I say it again, out loud when necessary, that He is good everywhere, even in the in between. I hum the tune through the rest of my ordinary week and I tense when I wonder if this is my "new normal." How can you slip back into a routine but remain forever changed? To go was never the hard part. To go and come back would be the challenge. But my word for the trip was *open* and the thing is, once you see the brokenness and the beauty, once you hear the cries and the laughter, you can never un-see or un-hear it all. You are forever responsible for what you have witnessed, forever given the charge of telling the stories.

When I looked deep and hard instead of turning away, what I saw staring back at me took my breath away. God's love story spans the globe and we are only one small line in the story, one swoosh of the brush and one piece of the puzzle.

I'm lit white-hot with words burning in my soul but He calls me to still my fingers and close my mouth. I flip the pages of the worn and torn and tearstained book and find my way to Colossians.

I keep reading the chapters every afternoon, unsure why I'm continually drawn to this particular book of the Bible. But then every single time my eyes find these seven words and I release a breath I don't even realize I'm holding, remembering the truth I've chosen to carry:

Christ in you — the hope of glory.

That's it. Right there.

The dark skin that brushed my arm is my brother. We found freedom in believing the words when the language wasn't our own and the glorious mystery sinks deeper into my soul: He is before all things and in Him all things hold together. We don't have to whisper the truth; we can sing it loud from the mountains.

My Birmingham, Gospel-broken heart says it again: He is God and He is good both here and there.

Worlds combine on a bench with three slats under a metal roof in Haiti and in a green car driving along Lakeshore and there is hope in the middle of it all.

I am here. Again.

I went there and came back here and then did it all over again. Now there's another song added to the mix, another tune stuck in my head just like Haiti is wedged in my heart. A song called *Holy Spirit* is following me around and chasing me down and I'm thankful every time it finds me because it helps me remember.[2]

So I sing it and raise my hands and I don't frankly care what the person next to me thinks — whether in a church building, on a highway, or in a classroom. The song is a popular one and so it splashes across radio stations often, but every time I'm convinced it is a gift just for me.

At least it was that one time in Haiti.

Standing in a conference room full of bloggers, argued about in a college classroom, while driving down the interstate, playing from my phone while I fall asleep or hummed quietly on the dirt streets of Haiti, this song has gripped my heart.

Flashback with me to a regular day this past March as I sat in my 9:15 Christian Theology class. Our topic of discussion was the Holy Spirit, which is laughable because there we were attempting to wrap words around Breath on a page.

But after taking a class in the fall on pneumatology, which is the study of the Holy Spirit, I was nearly beside myself to dig back into the part of the Trinity I never heard much about while growing up.

What I never saw coming, though, was getting into a "friendly discussion" over a popular song. Come to find out, my classmates thought it made no sense at all to sing a song about asking the Holy Spirit to come because, well, the Holy Spirit is already with us.

I don't know what came over me because I am not, mind you, the type of person to "start something" in class or to get into a heated debate. Especially with people I barely know on a topic — a Person — I'll never begin to even grasp a small percentage of. But then words were coming out of my mouth and I couldn't stop them, one after one tumbling out.

The room was quiet and not because of eloquence, but likely because I am not one to burst out and passionately defend a string of song lyrics in a classroom discussion. By that point in the semester it is obvious that I'm a thinker, a processor, and would rather ask questions than make statements.

But there we were. Well, there they were. I, however, was right back in Haiti with dirt between my toes. And *that* is why I could not stop the words.

The Monday morning of our second trip found us back in the village visiting with the people of Boukeron. Our team split up into three groups to go door-to-door collecting a census that would help us best partner with the people there. And so we walked. Mud house to mud house, person to person. We stopped at the first house on the left, and please understand that by house I don't actually mean house, but I know no other word except hut — and were immediately met with opposition. We asked the questions and received no answer save but a refusal to give information. We continued on the beaten path and the same thing played out again and again. As we left each house children, teenagers and a few adults began to follow several feet behind us.

Voices raised and the following turned to arguing. The sound of our voices faded as their words grew heavy and pointed. You don't have to know a language to understand deep inside that something is very wrong.

We weren't in danger but as a group of Haitian men started shouting something about our group and what we were doing, we each quietly slipped a few feet away. Two friends stood in the distance and started whisper-praying. I racked my brain for anything that would bring peace to the situation, but I only understood the tone, not the actual words being said, and so all I could offer was a silent *"God, I am so helpless here. I have nothing."*

My eyes searched the sky until I finally looked down into the eyes of a little girl in a dirt-covered pink dress. She didn't have a smile in sight but I reached my hand out, her mother eyeing me carefully. I could see the hesitation on her face and the dare in her eyes to walk further from the shouting, but there I was praying to the sky for bridges to be built and so out my hand went. I'm not sure if she took it or if I slipped my hand into hers as I knelt down to look into her face, but nonetheless my white skin was held in her brown hand and it was beautiful.

I don't remember her smiling for more than a split second, just a flicker of white, but it was something. The noise died down and we continued on as the little girl ran back to her mama. That was when I heard the music.

I couldn't pray more than, *"God I have no idea what to say. Just be here. You've got to come and be with us."*

Those sentences on repeat, not because He didn't hear me the first time but because I had nothing else. And then the notes played in my head and so I sang along. Not because He wasn't already in Haiti but because we desperately needed His presence. Not because my welcome would bring His power sweeping through but because it acknowledged the power already belonged to Him.

Quiet and timid, I whispered the lyrics under my breath. With every sentence I prayed along with the words, saying *"Lord, You alone can smooth the language barriers and bring peace to the chaos. We're here for You, only for You, always for You. I know You're already here, but come and sweep us up in Your love, power and truth."*

Over and over from house to house I hummed the tune. Sometimes the humming turned to singing and if you know me then you know that God performed a miracle right there in Haiti because as previously mentioned, this girl does not sing out loud.

Embarrassment, though, was the least of my worries. I didn't care about the theology of welcoming God to a place He already was and I didn't care that I was sing-asking for His presence while knowing He was right beside me. I couldn't pray the words and so I sang them.

Within an hour the same people who had been upset with our team were coming up to their cactus fences and inviting us inside. And somewhere in the in between, we had stopped by the houses of two witch doctors, the song always on my lips.

Later that evening I wrote the lyrics in my journal, followed by these words: *I tried hard to prayer-walk as we went around today but I didn't even know what to say.*

Maybe the lesson is to keep my ears and eyes open. I'm not sure — but I'm looking. Jesus is so sweet. And this place may be dark, but He keeps showing me the light.

And so yes, I had a few things to say in that American classroom because a Monday morning encounter in Haiti straight messed me up in the best way. When my words were few, He was found in abundance, His presence seeping through the mud-house cracks and overcoming language barriers.

A few months have passed and my memory is lacking, but to the best of my knowledge the classroom was dead silent as I said, "I love this song and here's why: I just returned from Haiti and in case you haven't been there, I want to tell you that there's a lot of darkness there. We hear about voodoo and we believe it's real but not fully, not completely. Because we haven't seen it with our own two eyes. But guys, I have. And I have to tell you, it's real. It is so real. But I also have to tell you that God is stronger. There is darkness, but He is brighter. And when Satan wanted nothing to do with us loving God's people in a small village in Haiti, when I was empty of prayers and completely helpless in actions, all I could do was sing this song. Not because the Holy Spirit wasn't there, but to acknowledge that He was. He doesn't show up when we sing, but don't you think He's so happy when we recognize His presence and say 'I want more of that'?"

In classrooms and on dirt roads hours from what we would deem civilization, may it solely be this:

God, may we become more aware of Your presence and Your goodness all around us, whether we're here or there or somewhere in between.

I write about Haiti with trepidation because I so long to honor the stories. I wait and relive the moments, my eyes scanning the words scratched in that little blue travel journal. I'm here now, but I'm still singing. I'm here and maybe one day my here will be Haiti, but for now I pen the words under an Alabama blue sky and I hum the tunes while saying one more yes to the in between.

JESUS IS

good and gracious,
mighty and merciful,
power and promise.

EVEN IN THE TIMES THAT FEEL
WILD AND VAST AND UNSURE,

he is there.

Chapter Seven

darkness & light

"Safe?"..."Who said anything about safe? 'Course he isn't safe.
But he's good. He's the King, I tell you." // C.S. Lewis, The
Lion, the Witch, and the Wardrobe

Of everyone in my friend group growing up and even all the way through high school, I was hands down the last person anyone would predict to go out and get a tattoo.

But I did.

Those three words right there will shock the pants off many of my real-life people reading these words because I didn't exactly make it known or go and tell the world. I didn't snap a picture and add a filter before posting or tweeting. I didn't make an announcement or write a blog post or anything big, although the tattoo was a big decision for me. In fact, this book is the first time I've written about it at all because that tattoo, it was for me and for Jesus. It is a constant reminder of truth on the bright days and the dark days.

For years I knew I wanted a tattoo but what I wanted and where I wanted it changed approximately every 6-8 months. On my wrist? A word in cursive lettering? A symbol by my ankle? As soon as I thought I finally had it nailed down, I would change my mind. And so I made a deal with myself. I decided that I couldn't get a tattoo of anything, anywhere, until I was happy with both the what and the where for at least one full year.

I may be stubborn and independent but I'm also Type-A and I'd like to believe I'm not stupid. If I couldn't stick with an imaginary tattoo for a year, I certainly shouldn't put anything permanent on my body just yet.

So I waited. I thought and prayed and read about how our bodies are the temple of the Holy Spirit. I would often draw something small with non-permanent black ink, but even when those little drawings looked all right, they weren't right. I couldn't put my finger on it, but no matter what the word or saying was at the time, something was off. What message did I want to place permanently on my body, a body that He has called His temple?

Three months after returning from my first trip to Haiti, I began experiencing night terrors. At the time, I had never even heard the term and so I thought I was just having really bad dreams. One of my earliest memories is of a nightmare that involves the witch from Snow White, a cliff, and a free-fall. Clearly, I am no stranger to weird nightmares. But these were different and they hung around like eyeliner that is still there the next day. You think you've scrubbed it all off but then you wake up and wipe the sleep from your eyes, only to discover your fingers are smeared with black.

The after-effects of these night terrors stuck with me and hung on even in the daytime. Unlike anything I had experienced before, I would go about my normal, ordinary life and yet feel as if a dark cloud was pushing me, pressing in and holding my wrists tight. The darkness wouldn't let go. I could feel myself slowly sinking, exhausted from what felt like endless nights of fighting for sleep, only to watch the morning light slip through the blinds as I would sigh and stand up for another day.

For the first time in years, everything seemed to be working well, like a well-oiled machine. My health was good, relationships were mended, and I was walking through life with community by my side and Jesus as my best friend. By and large, everything seemed like sunshine until suddenly I was thrown into the pitch-black dark.

I don't know about you, but one of the last things I want to be is a hindrance or an inconvenience. Asking for help is hard for me — especially when I don't know exactly what I'm asking for. I wasn't sure how to reach out or even what was going on inside, but I decided I wasn't going down without a fight and so I opened up the can of worms and trusted one of my people. Even though I didn't know what was going on in me, I knew I couldn't face the dark on my own any longer.

She asked me one question that flipped the switch and changed the fight.

"Do you think it might be spiritual warfare?"

Truthfully, I had wondered that myself but I would always dismissively wave away the idea. The words *spiritual warfare* are a big deal to me and not something that I believe should be thrown around willy-nilly. I believe there are angels and demons and that a fight is going on around us all the time, every day. And I believe you and I are part of that fight and that although the war has already been won through Christ Jesus, there are still daily battles waging around us.

But I thought and prayed. I searched His Word and clung to His promises like a raft in the raging sea. Every time I felt myself sinking down into the deep dark, it was as if Jesus blew life and air into the worn places, took my hand and said He'd walk with me on the water. He wasn't taking me to the shore or the safety of a boat, but instead calling me to fix my eyes on Him instead of the swirling unknown of the waves that the wind had suddenly tossed me into.

I gave it a name. I called it spiritual warfare.

It was dark, darker than the darkest dark I had ever known. Months later I hesitantly put one more word on it: depression. Just typing that here and seeing those letters written out in black have me feeling like I'm in a chokehold. The honest truth is that it was not pretty. I was not lovely or kind or any fun to be around. It was all I could do to fight for the light one more day.

For months I would reach my hand out, just like when you turn the lights off before climbing into bed. I couldn't see my hand in front of my face as I stumbled and walked hesitantly forward, but my hand found His reaching out for me. And so I walked in the dark but Jesus walked with me. I wasn't in physical danger, but my soul felt bound. So I began to search the Scriptures and read the Word as if my next breath depended on it because honestly, the battle seemed that fierce, that real. I yelled at Satan and asked two friends to daily bang the doors of heaven on my behalf. I stumbled and I fell but every day I would pull out the story of David and Goliath and I would read about the armor of God. There were pinpricks of light but mainly I was just learning to walk in the dark.

You can stand with hands raised in worship one day and kneel with hands over your face in frustration hours later. It is entirely possible to sing and smile on Sunday morning only to lay awake Sunday night with tears trickling into your ears, eyes staring straight upward, asking God once again to be near.

I don't care if you've gone to church every Sunday since you were in your mother's womb — darkness is real and it spares no one. Yes, even Jesus.[1]

Everything can be fine on the outside and you can be completely un-fine on the inside. It's pretty difficult to explain that one to the people around you, trust me. If you hear "What's wrong?" and "I don't know" is the only response you can manage, I just want to pause right here and tell you that is completely okay.

It's okay to not know where the heaviness has

come from as long as you know Who can carry it.

It's okay to be frustrated when you can't find the answers if you'll just hold tight to the only Answer.

It's okay to wrestle and fight if you lay there each night knowing He is fighting for you.

It's okay to not know how to answer the people around you if you know the only way to answer back to the darkness is to say one name: Jesus.

It turns out that even when you're walking in the dark you can still be walking with the Light. Darkness is not a punishment or even necessarily a test, but it is an opportunity to see Him shine so bright you'll be blinded in the best way. So whisper it when you're scared, when you're tired, and when you've got nothing left but Him. Shout it when you're angry and when you've got everything to fight for. Sing it when you're still, when you're in the battle, and when you've made it through one more day.

There isn't always a reason for the sadness or the heaviness. Sometimes walls go up and there's no explanation, but don't fight alone. Take the risk and let someone in. Allow them to help you tear the walls down and choose to fight together. Ask the ones you trust to bring your name before the throne daily until you're no longer drowning. But if that's too hard and you simply don't know how to manage any of it, not even one more thing, then this is what you've got to know: just say Jesus.

Repeat what you believe not because you've stopped believing but because there is power in His name. He is Light and the darkness must flee. Whisper how much you love the Father, offer praise to His Son who was crucified and then raised to life, and gratefully ask the Holy Spirit to intercede when you have nothing left to give.

Go ahead — talk to the darkness. Tell it what you believe and feel free to mention how the battle has already been won. Jesus comes out victorious, so keep on whispering His name.

The waves might continue to roll, the wind howling in your ears. Sometimes I couldn't shout over the noise of the storm or the heaviness of the dark, so I sang. Sometimes I didn't have anything left in me to sing, so I whispered. But I promise you, the darkness has to flee at the sound of His name.

Once I began to call it what it was, I knew I needed to prepare for the fight by putting on armor. I started to study both Ephesians 6 and the story of David and Goliath. Ephesians 6:13 tells us, "Therefore put on the full armor of God, so that when the day of evil comes, you may be able to stand your ground, and after you have done everything, to stand." It's funny, all this armor of God that is listed out for us to wear. The one thing that will pierce, the only weapon we are to wield, is the sword of the Spirit, which is the Word of God. As I read these words in the midst of my dark, I couldn't help but wonder why God would ask us to put on armor when sometimes we already feel so weighed down.

But there's an unexpected gift in showing up for your daily bread as you open the tear-stained pages. As I read and reread these passages, I learned that the tip of Goliath's spear weighed close to fifteen pounds and his armor was over one hundred pounds. David, completely armor-less and fighting with a slingshot and five stones, killed the giant with one shot.

Could it be that the armor of God is weightless, lifting the heaviness and placing it in His hands? Is it possible that as we open His Word, we are sharpening the tip of an invisible sword that is being used every day as we combat the darkness and the lies that swirl around us in an invisible battle?

God has already taken care of the ultimate outcome, but He is with us in the battle and He asks us to put on our armor, to stand up and walk. Some days that feels too big, too impossible, but the armor of God is a relief, not a burden.

Sometimes Goliath looks more like getting out of bed in the morning than a looming giant. Sometimes Goliath looks less like an enemy and more like asking for help. Sometimes Goliath simply looks like showing up and standing up and continuing to trust.

When everything is dark and you're in oceans deep, remember that He walks on the water and so you're not going to sink. There is hope in knowing that He brings beauty from ashes, light from dark, and life from death. This is who He is. This is what He does. And so we show up and stand up and raise our hands in worship, daring to whisper His name until sleep comes, believing that the darkness must take a step back because Light is with us.

I graduated with a Journalism and Mass Communication degree with a Print concentration and a minor in Religion. It's a mouthful, I know. I'll sum it up for you: I like to write and I love learning about Jesus.

If I could go back and do it all over again, I would switch my major and my minor. My apologies to the JMC department, y'all are great and really, it has nothing to do with you.

The thing is, a part of me that I didn't even know was dormant came alive in my religion classes. Would it better serve my career to have switched my major and minor? Probably not. But I showed up for every religion class excited, ready to learn, wrestling with questions and satisfied with not getting all the answers as long as I discovered more about the Answer. Learning about Jesus and pneumatology and the Filioque clause was completely overwhelming and thrilling. Every single class brought me back to my own smallness and His greatness.

So maybe you can understand why I love Hebrew and Greek. I never took either language because let's be honest, I was just trying to survive four semesters of Spanish. But as I sat under the teaching of those who have studied these languages and read the roots of the words found in the Word, I began to see so much meaning in Scripture that has been lost in the English translation.

Here's a fun tidbit for those who, like me, never knew: the Old Testament was largely written in Hebrew with a portion of it written in Aramaic, which was a similar but distinct language. It's kind of like saying something is written in both Spanish and Portuguese. Although different, they are sufficiently closely related so that a reader of either language would understand much of the other. The New Testament was written in *koine,* which is common Greek, understood by almost anyone at that time, whether educated or not. It was not high-class or complicated, but instead could reach far and wide.

During the fall of my senior year, I asked my parents to purchase a Hebrew and Greek keyword study Bible for my birthday. Every week I would lug that thing to bible study, eager to share cross-references and the root of each word in the Scripture we had studied the previous week. It became the best little game, this diving deep into the Word, into two languages I knew almost nothing about but my heart came alive in.

My tattoo is in Hebrew.

The words are pulled straight from the Old Testament, although you'll find them in the New as well. I chose Hebrew on purpose because the Old Testament holds a lot of unknowns and a lot of in betweens, but Jesus, He is coming. He is on the way. He is good and gracious and mighty and merciful. He is power and promise and even in the Old Testament times that feel wild and vast and unsure, He is there. He was always there.

You are not alone in the wilderness.

There's a man named Joshua and he's kind of a big deal in the Bible. I mean, the guy followed after Moses as the leader of the Israelites. You could say he had some big shoes to fill. There are several different stories of his trust in the Lord and his faithfulness to believe what God said, but there was that one time God said walk and Joshua did — and it was a little crazy, if we're being honest.

It isn't unusual to walk. Every day we walk through joys and struggles, through the dark and on into the light, but Joshua was leading the Israelites into battle and God said walk. Not "fight" or "prepare" or "bring sacrifices." He didn't ask them to write a blog post or tweet an encouraging verse or phone a friend.

Walk. Believe. Stay with it.

I don't know what battle you're walking into or the fight you're in right now, but I believe this word from God is for such a time as now. Spiritual warfare is real and if you don't believe me, just look for it around you. It's there. People are drowning all around us and more likely than not, some of your people are doing their very best to walk on the water and hold onto Jesus as best as they know how. It's been over a year and I'm still learning to walk in the dark. But there is great comfort in knowing that God did not leave His people in the wilderness and He has not left you in the desert to aimlessly wander in circles. The war has been won but the battle is still waging all around and as we walk in the dark, there are lessons to be learned.

Looking again at the story in Joshua 6, we see that the Israelites were going into battle against the city of Jericho but the gates were securely barred. No one went in or out. Essentially, everything was on lockdown. Do you ever feel that way? Like all doors are shut and you can't find an ounce of hope no matter which gate you come to?

Before a single thing was done, a single brick fallen from the city wall, a single step taken in battle, the Lord told Joshua, "See, I have delivered Jericho into your hands." Not I *will*, but I *have*.

From their eyes, the battle was just beginning. From God's perspective the glory was His and the battle was won. He is the God of Already's even when we're in the thick of it.

He tells them they'll win but still, they must have thought, "Okay, awesome. That's fantastic news and thank You so much. But if I may, how exactly do we go about this whole thing? It's great that we come out victorious but, umm, how?"

Walk. Believe. Stay with it.

He told them to march around the wall of Jericho in silence. Thousands upon thousands of people lined up to walk around the city wall. After completing their lap around everyone stopped and settled in for the night. Don't you just wonder what they were thinking?

"Y'all, nothing happened. Maybe God forgot?"

"I wonder if we misheard what God said..."

"Do you think we did it wrong? Maybe messed up somehow?"

"This is totally not how I saw this going down. Can we just do something now?"

Day after day after day.

Night after night after night.

They walked in silence and slept in the dark, only to get up the next day and do it all over again. It's not like a brick fell with every lap around. They didn't see any progress; it must have felt pointless. But they did it because God called them to it and His ways are good. They could have stopped on day four or five or six but thank goodness they kept on walking.

Because the walls fell on day seven.

Not one brick or a portion of the wall or a gate opening up. The entire wall all the way around the city just came crashing down. They let out a shout and in a way that only God could receive the glory, He won the victory. They kept walking; God did the winning.

Maybe you've been walking for months or years and taking one more step seems impossible. I may not know the battle you're facing but I know the One who can bring the walls crashing down. I know the One who walks on water, the One the wind and the waves obey and the One who asks for our trust and our declaration of love *even if not*.

In some ways, we're all learning to walk in the dark. Many of us are walking around and around again, praying for walls to fall and doing our best to obey even when there are more questions than answers. But listen to me and trust that I can say these words because I've felt the gripping, crushing weight of the dark and I have known the tender, gentle hand of the Light of the world:

It may be quiet for a while. You might lie in darkness and wonder what He's up to. But there is a day seven. Lace up your shoes. Don't stop walking. Don't give up. We don't know when the walls will fall but until God tells us anything different, we must keep on walking and believing. Do you hear the sound? The walls are crashing and Light is coming.

We sat facing each other, every chair looking toward the center. We held candles and I watched expectantly, waiting for the wax to begin dripping down. The lights were off, the room darkened, faces illuminated by flickering yellow.

One of the elders carried a large candle down the center aisle and as the light passed by, a slow tidal wave began as we blew each of our small, flickering flames out. Wisps of smoke went up and I felt tears sting my eyes.

It was dark.

And it's not so much that I'm scared of the dark, but that I'm worried about what it holds. I don't fear the night, but the quiet, the silence, and what could interrupt it. Sometimes it carries over into other parts of life too.

Cancer. Broken relationships. Depression. Unemployment. And yeah, spiritual warfare.

That Friday evening I knew I was perfectly safe. Surrounded by a church family who has taught me what the Body of Christ is supposed to look like, sitting in a room that has held me in several different emotional states through many seasons, I was both protected and secure. But it was dark. And it was Good Friday.

I don't know why Jesus did it. I wouldn't have. Oh, I've sat around and thought about it, sure. If everyone's eternal security all hung on me, would I go to the cross? Would I endure the pain? What if it were just for my people, the ones who carry my heart?

Honestly, I would not.

I would want to, yes. I would ache to be strong enough, brave enough, loving and courageous and a million other things. But I would not be.

We sang in the quiet and sat in the silence and the tears rolled down my face. I didn't even care. Because my Jesus, He did it for me. Inside I heard the nudge, that little whisper on a loop, telling me "for you, for you, for you. I love you, you, you."

And then we stood, one by one at first and then a massive, quiet, somber collection of people walking toward the cross in the dark. We individually picked up the black pieces of cloth that had been behind our backs the whole service, unnoticeable and maybe even a bit comfortable, and we walked the center aisle. Black in my hand, I shuffled toward the cross and all I had to offer besides my sinful self was "I'm sorry. Oh God, I am so sorry." In the background a child was wailing and it was all I could do not to join his lament.

I hung the cloth there. I left it, turned around, and walked out of the service and the church building into the light of a setting sun. Out of darkness, straight into light. Yet my face felt like plastic, that strange, tightened feeling that comes when tears roll down in streams.

The next day I drove to my favorite coffee shop and attempted to put words to what the day after Good Friday feels like. As I typed words like "silence" and "confusion" and "broken promises," I stared out the front window directly above my makeshift table. Either it was too small or I was too big because I

looked like an adult trying to squeeze into her kin-
dergarten desk. But the wood beneath my laptop was
smooth and the light was streaming in between the
white panes. I sat there for hours, desperate for the
light to wash over me.

Good Friday was so very dark two thousand years
ago but the truth of it is that many of us are in a
Good Friday chapter right now. Or maybe you've
just walked out of one and you're searching hard for
the light, pulling up too-big chairs to too-little tables
just so a little bit of it will splash across your face.

Someone told me once, way long ago in those
awkward middle school days, that we're all either
about to enter into a hard time, in a hard time, or
leaving a hard time. This was obviously incredibly
encouraging to my little heart. But it's true. We're all
going to face dark times. Some chapters are just ugly
and feel like nothing more than pain. Some memories haunt us in the night and we wake only to feel
the depth of the wound. We would do anything to
turn the page, to re-write the story, to edit, change,
and erase.

Anything. We would do anything.

Because this is not how it was supposed to be. This
was not the plan and there is no light left to see by.

It is dark.

It is empty.

You and I, we are raw and exposed, broken and
lonely and desperate for a hand to hold.

Do you whisper it, too? Have you raised your eyes
up to the heavens and quietly asked how much longer? Have you ever whispered "Is this going to end
and are You going to fix this? Is there a point to the

pain and also, God, where are You in all of this?

The season feels never-ending, the waves always crashing, the story like one long Good Friday, and you can't see any reason to believe Sunday is anything more than a myth.

Blow out a candle, your one source of light? No way.

Walk the aisle in the dark? Not a chance.

Approach the cross with nothing but weight on your shoulders and a mess in your hands? Never.

Yet He is there. Waiting. Patient. Worn and torn, bruised and bleeding, all for you and your broken, messy, bloodied heart.

You've been in a war and there may be light on the other side but you're not even sure the other side exists. So that center aisle, that path you're walking? The road you've been down, the pages you're turning, the story you're living? It's a mess of gravel and rocks and you, you're all cut up and exposed. You don't know where to carry the light because you can't even find it. But He is there. For you and with you and carrying you one step further, even when the darkness is surrounding and suffocating. He hasn't gone anywhere. Even on Good Friday.

Blow out your little light. Watch the wisps of smoke float away and then pick up the black cloth of your mess. Step forward. Carry it in your hands, shuffle toward the cross, and offer it to Him, yourself to Him.

He will not turn away. You are not too much. Your mess is not too messy, your heart not too broken, your story not too ugly. He is waiting and He is good.

Walk another lap and look up toward the sky on

your day five and six and again on day seven. It's never too late for Light to break through. It will come streaming in. Just a pinprick at first, a small glimmer of hope, one minute that you forget the sadness, a day or two of breathing easier.

In her book *Learning to Walk in the Dark*, Barbara Brown Taylor beautifully says that "Even when light fades and darkness falls — as it does every single day, in every single life — God does not turn the world over to some other deity. Even when you cannot see where you are going and no one answers when you call, this is not sufficient proof that you are alone."[2]

Even when you cannot see a way, cannot catch a breath, cannot stop the hurry and rush and panic inside. Even then and even if not. Hold fast because Light is here and Light is coming and your sky is going to blow up golden and bright. And then the sun will set again and night will come as it does every single day. But that is how it goes and we don't know how many more rounds we'll go. Sunrise, sunset. Sunrise, sunset.

I think that's the beauty of it. Would we fully appreciate the Light if we had never known the dark?

The Hebrew language reads right to left. This is important to me because the tattoo that was scratched into my right foot says four little words in the English language:

Out of darkness, light.

But when you read it in Hebrew, when your eyes see those words and you go from right to left, the very last word your eyes will land on is *light*. It is the closest word to my toes and so with every single step I take, light is guiding the way. I am stepping out of darkness into light.

Over and over His Word says these words, and so when I sent the translation of the phrase taken from a verse in the Old Testament to one of my religion teachers, I was floored when he replied, "As with everything, context is key. But the translation you have says literally, 'from the midst of darkness, light.'"

And then I cried.

In the midst of the hazy mist of questions and sickness, in the broken and lonely places, when I feel small and unseen and my heart is torn between here and there, in the darkest of nights, He is there.

In the swirling dark, I clung to the promise that Jesus is the light of the world and so although I couldn't see the light at the end of the tunnel, because Jesus was with me I was walking through the dark with Light holding my hand.

In the darkest night, there was still light.

You know, light always comes because Light always wins.

The night can be holy too, but we still light the candles and hold our breath, keeping watch through the night for dawn to break. It will. It does.

Before you turn the page, I want to truthfully tell you that although I'm walking into the light, there is still darkness. The battle continues but I just keep saying His name and proclaiming that Light is greater. I'm confident that we may not always see the outcome of our prayers, but prayer keeps things from us and gives things to us that otherwise would not be. So I keep on praying and proclaiming and praising. I put on the armor and soak in the Word so I can pick up the Sword. And when the waves loom large in the distance I look down at the words etched into my skin, this temple of the Holy Spirit, and I remember walking toward the cross with black ink marking me as I laid the black cloth on the rough wood. The ink on my foot was only one day old as I approached the cross, thinking of the One who took on scars and marks, bruises and beatings on my behalf.

One day there won't be darkness, but until then may we rely on Him on Fridays, cling to His promises on Saturdays and celebrate Him on Sundays.

And when the week begins and we forget, when the things stack up and the thoughts of Him slip our minds, may we look again to the cross, remember the blood poured out for us, and offer our thanks. May we walk in His light and follow His steps, depending on the bread and the wine and His bride. May we approach the cross with joy instead of shame and trust instead of fear, acknowledging the dark and proclaiming that Light is greater still.

May we be slow to forget and quick to remember that it is finished. And all of us, voices raised together, hands reaching out and feet shuffling in the dark, may we say on day two and on day five and every other day that comes: light could break through but we'll keep on walking in the dark, trusting His heart for us, even if not.

There is purpose right here, right now, today.

Chapter Eight

names & dreams

The seasons change and you change, but the Lord abides evermore the same, and the streams of His love are as deep, as broad, and as full as ever. // Charles Spurgeon

I don't want you to know this part of me.

One of my favorite quotes about writing is by Flannery O'Connor. She said, "I write because I don't know what I think until I read what I say." I'm pretty sure that in the process of writing this chapter, I am about to discover just what I think about names and dreams, hopes and longings and the truth that this ampersand season might last a whole lot longer than anticipated.

I never set out to write these words, to tell you about these dreams that sometimes hurt, but then again I never planned to write this book. But God tapped my shoulder in that way of His, the one where you know you have a choice as to whether or not you'll obey, but you also know good and well that you wouldn't dare to disobey. And so you'll do it, whatever it is. Even if you'd honestly rather not, obeying is the most important thing because you love Him and trust His heart for you.

That is the mental space I was in as I began this

book. Everything was going smoothly, the words coming naturally, until one morning as I made breakfast He tapped my shoulder one more time and spoke so clearly words I know to be His because I would never come up with them myself.

Tell that story.

Share that space.

You've gone deeper, go deeper still.

You've written with your heart, now write in the middle of the hurt. Practice not knowing the answers and be gut-level honest with the questions. I will be real, I will be present, and I will be more than enough. I can take it. But I need you to go there and put it down in ink, although that seems scariest of all, because there is someone else who needs these words. Will you do that for Me? Will you tell your story and give Me the glory?

With shaking hands and tears blurring the keyboard, I will. Every single word found in this book matters to me. Each one holds weight, every in between and ampersand season has had its own unique challenges and joys, hardships and victories. And yet they all, in one way or another, have closure.

I am okay without knowing all the answers. I have experienced healing, seen broken places become mended spaces, been found by community and discovered my own smallness in light of His greatness. I am learning to be both here and there and most days, the light is shining through just a little bit brighter.

Although I am still in the in between of each of these, if every chapter were a pendulum I would be swinging toward the right, into the healing and the light.

But not with this one.

I am smack in the middle, at times feeling stuck and at other times totally free. Daily I am wrestling to live with joy while trusting Him in the middle of this ampersand.

You and I may never meet and I can't begin to list out your deepest desires and dreams. But if you believe, as I do, that God knows every piece of you and is completely in the know when it comes to what you long for, and if you believe, as I do, that in His love for you He placed those desires inside and has the ability to gift you those things, would you still love Him and trust His heart if, although He could grant your heart's deepest desires, He chose not to?

Would you still believe God is good? Would you still trust His loving kindness toward you?

Could you look around in your ampersand and say "I know You could heal and mend and bring things to be that You placed as dreams within me, but I will love You even if not"?

I couldn't tell you what I had for breakfast yesterday, but I can tell you where I want to be a week, three months, or five years from now.

I am a planner. I chart and color-coordinate spreadsheets because I want to. Part of the fun of it all, no matter the length of the road trip or the project I'm beginning, is to dream and plan and make lists.

I have a list notebook, for goodness sake. And yes, that's exactly what you would imagine it to be — a book full of list after list of anything imaginable.

There aren't many memories from childhood that have stuck with me, but I've never forgotten a conversation with Nana where I likely was planning some surprise or adventure and she responded with a half-smile as she quietly said, "Kaitlyn, don't forget the lesson found in Proverbs 16:9. We can make our plans, but the LORD determines our steps."

Let's be honest, I didn't like that very much.

What was so wrong with a grand adventure? Back then they were innocent, last minute plans to play in the backyard or swim at a neighbor's pool, but even at a young age a piece of me went against the idea that my plans could be anything less than the best.

It's not like I was planning anything *wrong* at the age of seven. Fast-forward and it's not like interviewing for post-graduation jobs is a bad thing to do. It is not a terrible idea to have a dream or a goal and work towards it.

But I've learned that in my planning I often place control in my hands and responsibility on my shoulders, when the world is not on my shoulders but in His capable hands. The story of my life is mine, yes, but I've placed it in the hands of the Author, so why do I scribble notes in the margins and rush ahead to write the next chapter?

Most of us have big dreams for the future, goals we want to reach and hopes that scare the living daylight out of us. And listen, I think that is more than okay. Dreaming can be some of the scariest, bravest hoping we ever do.

Nana's lesson was never "don't dream, Kaitlyn" but instead "when you dream, remember Who is already there in the future you're imagining."

If you don't know just where you're going, join the party. If you have dreams and aren't sure how to reach them, welcome. Someone somewhere once said that it isn't so much about the destination as it is about the journey, and so maybe it's not so much about the knowing but the going.

Steady. Faithful. Trusting. Believing one step at a time that although He has the best plan, He is also the Giver of dreams.

Right now, my ampersand is my name. This is not at all convenient if I were to, you know, attempt to forget or move out of this in between season. My name goes with me everywhere. This particular dream may not be yours, but substitute your deepest desire in place of me and my name and you'll understand.

I want to change my last name. I was never the girly girl child who loved tea parties, who then grew into the teenager that loved high heels and makeup, who later became the college student who purchased bridal magazines. I can barely stand the color pink and I can't curl my hair to save my life. I do, however, wear makeup multiple times throughout the year: Easter, my birthday and Christmas.

I think we can all agree that no one would use the

words "girly girl" when describing me, but that has never once stopped me from wanting to be both a wife and a mother.

I have big aspirations, dreams and goals and things I want to accomplish. I want to see the world, experience other cultures, dare and risk and go on adventures. But I also long to be a good wife and a loving mother. I want to chase after my passions but it's just as important to me that I passionately love my family.

The thing is, I am single as all get out.

And truthfully, I am okay. Actually, I am more than okay. I love my life and these days and I am doing my very best to take every moment for what it is, look at it like an opportunity, learn more about myself and sink my roots deeper into God. He is more than enough and I truly am satisfied in Him. But that doesn't mean the dreams have disappeared. Unless God answers them or takes them away, I'm quite certain they're here to stay.

Before you start talking back to me via the page in your hands, let me quickly say just a few things. I am completely aware that I have "more time" and there is "no rush" and I should "enjoy these days because I won't get them back."

I know these things and I wholeheartedly agree with each of them.

But that doesn't take away the longing. It doesn't stop the ache. It does not, for one single second, squelch the hope that is burning inside. I believe that He made me this way, that He built me and wired me to nurture and to love. It is not a coincidence that my friends call me Mom.

If someone were to come along and tell you that you should enjoy the days before your dream comes to fruition because one day you'll want this time back, if they were to say that you shouldn't rush or worry or wonder but instead be satisfied with what you have, wouldn't you want to maybe-kinda-sorta pinch their cheeks? Because really, people, this is not kind. This is not helpful, no matter the dream. And yet we both know that someone who appears to have what you dream about will, at one point or another, look back and say, "Oh, if only I could go back to where you are. You don't know how good you have it."

Here is what I've decided: there are challenges on both sides of every mountain. The grass is not greener on the other side; the grass is greener wherever it is watered and tended to. And so I'd like to kindly say, friend, you tend to your grass and I'll tend to mine. I'm going to water the heck out of the single life, using every ounce of time to chase Him with my whole heart, to fix my eyes on Him and not a single thing around me, and to fall in love with the One who made me and placed these dreams inside. And I'm going to do each of those things while believing and trusting and hoping and praying for the dreams He's placed within me to come to life. I will be present in the ampersand.

We've got to stop looking at another person's grass and longing for what they have, even when it is what we want, and instead tend to what God has placed right under our own two feet.

In the midst of this, while watering the grass He has me standing on right now, I have started to tell

Him my dreams. Not because He doesn't know and not once as a reminder in case the God of the universe forgot, but because He is a safe place. He understands every single piece of me.

He has been there at the weddings where I dance and clap and am filled with joy. He is there as I scroll through social media and feel my stomach drop as my eyes see the seventh engagement announcement in as many days. He is there every time someone asks "have you met a guy yet?" and He sees the struggle as I try to find words to a question that unintentionally sounds like both an accusation against my worth as an individual and a caution that all of life is a waiting game until a significant other enters the picture. He placed the desire to mother children and to love and care for another inside of me, and so these dreams are of no surprise to Him.

I take them to Him and I place them in His hands and I try to leave them there. Sometimes I take them back out and offer suggestions, like maybe if this just happened...? and what if You...? maybe this would help...?

But I am not God, and all the people said amen.

I pray a lot, and it isn't because I'm super spiritual but because He meets me there. He says He can carry the weight and the dreams and the hopes and the wonderings. He'll take it all because none of it is too much. God says He will carry my dreams carefully and I trust that to be true.

I do not, however, know if He will fulfill them. And that, that is where I lose my footing and feel my voice wavering, my hands trembling, because what if not? What if this is His plan and His heart for me is to draw me close and closer still as I place my dreams in His hands and choose Him? Everything could change tomorrow but perhaps it never will, and that is where I wrestle.

Will I say "even if not?"

Some days I do not.

Some days I want it all so badly that I can almost taste it, my mind becoming consumed and wrapped up in an imaginary tale. It is normally right about then that He interrupts and asks if I will still praise His name if He doesn't change my name.

This is so very hard. But I trust with everything in me that He is for me. I believe that He is good in the beginning and at the end and on every single page in between. I am certain that God does not make mistakes and so I am confident that He has me exactly where He wants me. I am not even one centimeter off course because He is the guide. He will not lead me the wrong way. He will not keep from me what is best for me.

And so the only answer is that right now, in this space and at this time, this is His very best for me.

Right now, where you are at this very moment, you are surrounded by God's very best for you. There is nothing lacking. He won't be running to His heavenly storehouse like parents on Christmas morning who say, "Oh! I forgot that I hid something in the upstairs closet! Hold on, I'll be right back."

No, we've already got it all.

At the risk of sounding cliché, I have found it to be true that in Christ, we have all we need. We are lacking no good thing and nothing is missing.

What we're hoping and longing for, praying and

dreaming about, might be right around the corner. But where we are right now is God's very best for us in this very moment. When it is the exact right time, He will move the pieces on the board, connect the dots, or lead us elsewhere.

And maybe for me that will mean changing my name. Maybe for you that will be a child or a medical discovery or a contract or a phone call.

I keep laying this dream down and giving it up to Him, but that doesn't mean I'm giving up on it. Instead, I am looking around at what He has given and calling it more than enough because, well, it is.

My life is not paused. I am not saying "hold please" to the rest of my dreams. I was never the ballerina on stage as a child but I was absolutely the girl with her nose in a book. Even before I enjoyed writing, I imagined what it would be like to see my own name printed on a book cover.

But I never once pictured the word *Bouchillon* in print. I was certain that by the time I began writing a book, if that even happened one day, I would surely be married. Because that's how life goes, right? High school, college, job, engagement, marriage, baby. In my mind, the job and the engagement steps had the possibility of switching places, but a book only factored in somewhere after the marriage stage.

And yet you're holding a book in your hands and printed on the cover in gold you'll find my name, Kaitlyn E. Bouchillon. It might be different one day, but it would have been rather silly to put one long blank line in place of my last name.

We often live in the ampersands but God is not playing a game with our lives. God is not on a road trip holding a game of MadLibs in His hands and randomly assigning this and that and the other to each of us. He has a plan and it is a good one. There are no blanks in His story and so I refuse to draw one into my pages.

My ampersand is my name and I will carry it with as much grace as I can muster. And when I struggle to believe and have faith, I'll look to Jesus and say "Lord, I believe, help my unbelief." I might sit for a while and read the words of Paul, who urged us to run our own race and who allowed prison to become his pulpit, writing letters that would reach generations of people who were locked up themselves. His race didn't look like what he had imagined, but there was great purpose every step of the way.

I'll likely smile as I think of Jesus, Son of God and single on earth. And then I'll wipe my eyes or write another page or go out with friends or something, anything, that is choosing to live.

If God doesn't make mistakes, and He doesn't, then God doesn't waste or erase a single line in any of our stories. There is purpose right here, right now, today. I want to get a little crazy and choose to live in faith in the ampersand. I want to dare to say that He is the greatest treasure, better than every hope or dream or longing inside.

Fear often tries to ride the coattails of our dreams. For me, this looks like doubts and darkness, lies and wonderings of whether I am enough, if something is "wrong with me," and what the purpose is in these days. There are times when I feel small and lonely and stuck. Although I am not jealous of those who have a boyfriend, are engaged, or are married, I long for it myself. And then fear enters in and says those things aren't for me. Fear says I will never get there. Fear dares to rear its head and raise its voice, loudly proclaiming "keep on wishing, girl" and quietly whispering "you better just get used to how it is now."

Fear sounds a whole lot like Satan.

But do you know what happens when you listen to the Voice of Truth and then pass His messages along? For starters, Satan gets really annoyed. The darkness might get darker, the lies louder. That's okay though because I'm just over here shouting the truth over myself, singing His praise and speaking His name into the places inside that feel bare and exposed, lonely and thin, unsure and weak.

If the lies are going to pour down, then the Truth is going to have to rain down, too.

Colossians 2:7 tells us to grow our roots deeply into Him and to let our lives be built on Him, promising that the after-effect will be that our faith will grow strong in the truth we were taught and we will over-flow with thankfulness.

He will teach us the truth. He will show us the way. God will be faithful to these things because after all, He is the way, the truth, and the life. He longs to give us more of Himself.[1]

When God asks me to trust what He knows more than what I can see, I must rely on His sight and let the water that rises wash me clean instead of sweep me over. And isn't it funny, because the water that floods is the very same water that brings nutrients to the roots.

God knows it because I've told Him so: If life is a flowerbed then the truth is I love the Gardner but I don't always love the garden. I am learning to live and love in the in between, but often I am bent over with petals flat on the ground as the gardening hose drenches day after day.

I am a sopping wet mess of dreams and hopes, but the roots are growing deeper. The water is still pouring and then soaking wet I look up and remember He is the Living Water and it all makes sense, how He is with me in it all, always loving and kind and in the middle of the storm, He is the Living Water that walks on water and so yes, I will bloom right where I am planted, trusting that the very rain that washes over me is pulling me down to my knees, closer to Him.

Let petition and praise shape what you see as a problem into a prayer.

I repeat those words and I hold them up next to Good Friday, the very darkest day that was necessary for the very best day to arrive.

Because we have the gift of time, you and I both know that we can breathe easy on Friday because Sunday is coming and all will be well. But on that long-ago Saturday? When the world was dark and tears never stopped flowing, mixing with the blood poured? As they longed to go to the tomb but weren't able, as they gathered together in upper rooms, confused and some doubting, full of pain and grief spilled over? They were in the in between.

If we could go back in time and talk face-to-face, I would reach for their hands and shake their shoulders, shouting with everything in me that it will be okay. I would tell them to just hold on, to wait a little longer, to have faith and believe.

But they didn't realize. They didn't remember the promise. They couldn't see Sunday was coming.

Sunday healed what Friday broke and Saturday wept over. Sunday redeemed what Friday lost and Saturday couldn't see past.

But they didn't see Sunday; they were living in Saturday.

I can't help but wonder if God ever speaks these words over me and over you, whispering love and shouting truth, reminding us that Sunday is coming and death does not have the final say, that our dreams are not a long-shot and our hopes, when rooted in Him, have a sure foundation.

To the disciples, the story seemed all but over.

When our dreams feel out of reach and we live as if we're shuffling through, life paused until He answers, we are essentially choosing to unpack our bags and move in permanently to a season of Saturday.

And I know our world acts like Saturday nearly every day of the year. We live in a broken, painful, confusing world. Chaos is all around us and so many things can fall apart. Sickness, pain, broken hearts, death. All of it, Saturday. We can't see Sunday down the road. There seems to be no hope amidst all our anger and hurt.

But Sunday is coming. God has not paused His plans and so let's not pause our lives. Sunday might not look like what we're longing for or dreaming about, but that doesn't change the fact that it is coming and it will be better than we could hope for. The book didn't end on Friday or Saturday; God simply turned the page.

He loved you in your Friday of yesterday, in your darkness and pain. He holds you in the confusion and silence of Saturday. And friend, He is coming for you on Sunday. Hold on. He will not delay. His timing is perfect, His promises true. He will come through.

Nothing is impossible, every chain is breakable, and all of heaven was just practicing their counting.

3.. 2.. 1..

It has always been this way. A word shows up everywhere in my life for weeks on end for what appears to be no reason at all. Suddenly it is on every social media feed, the topic of several podcasts I listen to, and mentioned in conversations with friends and strangers alike.

At first it seems like a coincidence and I never get to pick the word, of course, but He keeps speaking to me this way because finally I am paying attention.

You know how people say "Get with the program"? I am with the program.

Right around January, thousands of people choose to focus on one word for the coming year. Instead of making resolutions, they look for and incorporate one particular word into their lives. Although God continues to give me one word, it never comes knocking on the first day of the year. But since God keeps using one word to get my attention, and because I break every New Year's Resolution by mid-February, I figured I would try it.

In 2013 I chose *beloved*. Be loved. Be love. Be the beloved.

But then the calendar flipped to 2014 and I grasped at straws. I'm a word-lover and I couldn't choose. Eventually, February came and I landed on *believe*. It seemed like a good one, considering 2014 would mean beginning my final year of college and living out the friendship miracle of dry bones living once again.

It was a good word. It fit well and reminded me to believe His promises. But then summer hit and the darkness came. *Believe* took on a whole new meaning.

Believe there is light when all you can see is the dark. Believe the truths you know to be true when all you hear are lies. Believe the promises. Believe He will carry you through. Believe there will be no more weeping or pain or sadness. Believe Light has already come. Believe there is space at the table for you. Believe that believing is not a mistake.

I clung to the word that was just a passing thought in February, and I believed. All of it. Even when it didn't make sense or add up, I chose to believe what I knew to be true in the light when everything just seemed dark.

I thought about the previous Christmas and how the word floating around my brain, printed in ink on all the book pages, playing on the radio no matter which station I turned to, was *Emmanuel*. God come down to us, God with us, God coming back for us.

I was fascinated by the word, by the God who would come for me, stay with me, and come for me once more. I knew this God-man but I wanted to know Him more, to know Him fiercely. Emmanuel, my word for the season. Emmanuel, God with me in every season.

Believe. Emmanuel. Believe.

I began to ask questions like: Where do we make space in our schedules for the Savior who came as a baby to redeem a broken people? And how do we ask that question honestly when the question itself makes us want to curl up in shame?

"Make space" for Jesus? It seems absurd that we would have to work at making space for the King of Kings. But take a quick look at my planner and it's clear that things are busy and life moves quickly by.

We have to make space in the pace. We have to have Emmanuel there because without Him, Christmas and every single other day is just a climbing of ladders and a bending of the back to reach one more rung and sow one more seed on a planet that was never meant to be our permanent home.

When we make a little space in our pace for Emmanuel, our pace becomes peace.

God with us in the hurry, the hectic, and the to-do list. While cooking dinner and going out with friends, God with us at the table. In the making and the dreaming, in the encouraging and the writing and the cleaning, even there, God with us.

God come to us — believe.

God with us in the everyday ordinary — believe.

God coming back for us — believe.

Oh, how He loves us. We can always believe because God is always coming for His beloved, always returning to us and loving us. You are never too far gone, never too much or too little or not quite enough. You are not too lost or too hopeless. He came, He chose to call us His home, and He's coming back because the love of God is always coming for the lost, the unsure, the confused and sick and hurting, for the ones in the dark, for His children.

He used *believe* to remind me that we are not called to be a people who believe in what we can see, but a people who trust the Giver of dreams, the Light in the darkness, and the One who will always come for us, whether as a baby or as the King of Kings.

As the next year rolled around, I started making a list of words early on. I knew God would work through what I chose, and so I sat down and thought about what the coming year might hold and what I wanted to keep on the forefront of my mind. I listened and waited, hoping to sense what word I should choose for 2015. There were six options that seemed appropriate, each of them encouraging and also challenging. Although I figured they would each have a turn based on all my carefully laid out plans, God interrupted my ordinary, daily life and invited me into His plan.

I tried to fight it, if we're being honest, because option five on my list of words felt promising.

But then I made the mistake of saying it out loud, the word He chose for me for 2015, and I knew deep in my soul I couldn't avoid it if I tried.

Watch. In so many ways, that one word sums up every chapter in this book, every moment of living in the in between, knowing He could change things, and trusting He will be good even if not. As I write these words, it is October of 2015 and I'm still watching. I am looking for Him in my hopes and dreams and trusting that He'll carry my name for me. This isn't an in between to Him, it is simply part of the story.

Whatever your dreams are and whatever page you find yourself on today, I am confident that His words for me are also for you. He sees your deepest desires, the ones He planted in you, and He loves you more deeply than you'll ever know. His heart is for you and with you, but will you believe it? He could give you every one of your heart's desires, but if He chooses not to and instead simply gives you Himself, will that be enough?

I'm watching for Him in the middle pages. Today I will say "even if not." And when He asks again tomorrow, my prayer is that those three words will escape my lips again and again and the next day, too. In response, I hear these words spoken over me and to me, for me and also for you:

Keep your eyes open, wait and watch because I am a promise-keeper. I will watch to see that My own Word is fulfilled. None of this depends on your color-coding, love. I will provide all that is needed so when you have one hundred questions just watch for the Answer and follow it. Follow Me.

I am watching over you, over your coming and your going. I am with you in every season. Choose to water the grass under your own feet. When it comes to your people and when you want to be the one watching, when there are times that your voice shakes and your chin quivers and your arms refuse to let go of the ones you love or the season you're in, remember that although you can't always be everywhere, I will keep watch over the ones who hold your heart. I will be there, too.

And then, love, watch Me blow your mind in all the big ways and in the small, too. Watch for the daily joys and watch for the light in the struggles. Dwell in my Word, trust Me with the dreams I've given you, and breathe deep of the Peace in the pace. Love deeply, my girl. Enjoy the journey. Keep watch and believe.

TOO OFTEN
WE COMPARE
OUR BEGINNING
TO SOMEONE
ELSE'S MIDDLE
AND OUR OWN
BEHIND-THE-
SCENES TO
ANOTHER'S
HIGHLIGHT REEL.

Chapter Nine

live & tell

*There is no greater agony than bearing an
untold story inside you. // Maya Angelou*

Every life tells a story, each of us a character in a
story grander than our wildest imaginings. God's story comes out in our stories and just like dandelions,
stories spread farther than we'll ever know when we
breathe out and share.

As ordinary or messy as it may seem right now,
God is weaving pieces together that will tell of His
faithfulness when generations to come read the pages of your life. I want to leave a legacy that keeps the
rocks from making noise.

Luke 19:40 says that if we stay quiet, if we don't tell
of what God has done in our lives, the stones along
the road will burst into cheers. Although it's an incredibly strange mental image, possibly because I
somehow imagine hundreds of rocks doing the wave
while screaming and shouting, I don't want this to
ever happen.

If the rocks start crying out we have a serious problem on our hands. God is going to be praised and He
has said that if we don't tell our stories and give Him
the glory, the rocks are going to make a whole lot of

noise.

I know choosing to tell of His faithfulness can be hard when you're swirling somewhere in the deep dark and no one sees the broken places inside, but it was by going through my worst nightmare that I saw the beauty of His constant presence.

God has never once been anything but faithful to me, but I didn't truly see it until community fell apart and He picked me up. The scattered pieces of dreams and heartache fell into every space in my life, but slowly He glued the pieces back together. And then in His own timing, after writing a few more chapters and turning a couple more pages, He put the glue stick away and with tattered wings I flew into the arms of community.

I built so many walls and all along He was standing there saying, "Love, I have already taken the nails for you. Put the hammer down and let Me tend to your scars. I know what those feel like and I will not turn away."

I see Him on every page of my story and I don't know why that continues to surprise me because His was the hand holding the pen.

I fell in love in the summer of 2013, but it isn't what you think.

I fell in love with the power of story.

I couldn't escape it and suddenly the word was everywhere I went, this unshakeable burden to carry the power of story burrowing deep inside my soul.

God began to speak the truth to me, the girl with too many rocks in her pockets and the one who was only just beginning to believe in love again. This is what He told me:

It doesn't matter who you are or who you've been, every single person has a story. The artist, the CEO, the mom, the single college girl, the homeless man on the sidewalk, the cashier and the pianist. Every person is a walking story and when you keep your story to yourself, whether out of shame or fear or a belief that you don't have one to begin with, you are denying Me glory. There is power in every story, no matter what you have or have not walked through. I am there, I am writing, and I am asking you to live and tell the story I give.

It's not about us or the words that come out of our mouths or splash onto computer screens, it's about where the words come from and the One who gives them to us. Every story is a miracle and as C.S. Lewis has said, "Miracles are a retelling in small letters of the very same story which is written across the whole world in letters too large for some of us to see."[1]

You are loved today, yesterday, and forever by the greatest Author and it doesn't matter how much life you've lived or what you've walked through, He has given you a story.

When the final page is turned, a gravestone will be marked with two sets of dates. No matter who you are, we each get two dates and a dash in between and that dash becomes our story. Inside that thin line there are struggles and heartaches, mistakes and relationships and redemption, failures and accomplishments. We only get one dash and one story but it's up to us to live and tell it well.

The power of Jesus in your messy, bruised and bloody, confusing and in-process story could set someone free. There's that famous saying, those words about how Christians have the Cure and who in their right mind would keep the cure to cancer hidden and locked away from cancer patients? And so how can we sit down or shut up about a Love that loves all, includes all, frees all? How can we stay silent and continue believing our story isn't a miracle and a gift, even when we can't see how everything will shake out and we're walking in the in between?

When we lay hold of the truth that every story matters, we'll begin to see and believe that our story is included in the "every" story. And then we'll have to realize that although we haven't done the writing, it *is* our job to do the storytelling. It really isn't about us. It's not about me or you; it isn't about what chapter we're in or how "big" our stories are. It's all about the One who holds the pen.

Please don't wait until you've got it all figured out and life looks beautiful and put-together. That day is likely never to come, but God is there right now, right where you are, on the very page you're living.

There are entire chapters in my story that I wish I could scratch out and there are pages I've loved so deeply that I've underlined and dog-eared them. But this is my story, all of it, the broken and the mended, the darkness and the light, and I can't help but share. It's a jumbled, beautiful, unedited, unfinished and raw work in progress, but it is my story all the same. The world needs my story; the world needs your story. Will you tell of His faithfulness and goodness in the pages He has given you to live?

Stories are one of the most powerful things we'll ever come across. They can give deep joy, move us to action, and bring us to tears — all in the span of a few moments. Words strung into sentences, sentences into paragraphs, and paragraphs into chapters that turn into books take us to places we could never go otherwise. Opening the pages of a book is like entering into a new world.

You are made up of atoms but I am convinced that those atoms tell a story. You are a living, walking, breathing story. Every page counts, every sentence matters, and the question is not if you have a story but what you'll do with the story you have.

Will you let others read the pages? Will you welcome them in? Will you say "even if not" to the Author and then go one step further and tell the story He has given you to live? What will you do in the dash?

We don't need another person denying her story in favor of living another's. We don't need another story to go untold because of doubts or swirling thoughts that someone else's story is bigger, better, funnier, more interesting, or sure to make a greater impact.

The story of your life is yours alone and if you don't live it, no one else will.

Every day you choose to show up to life and love

deeply, every time you open up your mouth to tell the truth of what's going on, you share a chapter with us. Your one wild and beautiful life is the story of your days and we need it something fierce.

But we need you to fiercely love it, too, so turn your eyes away from the stares or the stats and listen to the Truth.

While it's true that someone could have similar circumstances and life experiences, no one can tell the stories that you have to tell because no one else sees the world in the way that you do.

We need you to live and love like your story matters, and then we need you to tell it. We need your words, your stories from the ampersands that declare that God is good and God is God, even if not.

There are those who will walk where you have walked and stand where you have stood and they are desperate for your story, for your truth and honesty, for your declaration that God is there every step of the way.

Maybe your life is nothing like what you expected. Maybe you've been bruised black and blue, you're drowning in the dark, or you feel too small to be noticed at all. Maybe you're living in the in between and you don't want to be there. But these days, they are part of your story. He has given you these chapters to live, He has authored these pages, and every single one matters.

He's the One writing but He asks you to do the telling.

Several years ago I read a quote from *Chasing Francis: A Pilgrim's Tale* that continues to guide me as I live, love, and learn in the in between seasons. In part of the book, the following conversation takes place: "Do you know the story of Rabbi Zusya?" he asked. "He was a Chasidic master who lived in the 1700s. One day he said, "When I get to the heavenly court, God will not ask me, Why weren't you Moses?" Rather, he will ask me, "Why were you not Zusya?"[2]

The man then continued: "Churches should be places where people come to hear the story of God and to tell their own. That's how we find out how the two relate. Tell your story with all of its shadows and fog, so people can understand their own. They want a leader who's authentic, someone trying to figure out how to follow the Lord Jesus in the joy and wreckage of life. They need you, not Moses," he said.[3]

I really don't need you to be Moses.

But I desperately, achingly need you to be you.

It's easy to look at the people in our iPhones and on computer screens and in our daily lives and think, "If only I could be more like her. If I read my Bible more, prayed more, or did something big, bold, and brave like so and so did, maybe I would have a story worth telling."

You are only called to be you, I am only called to be me, and neither one of us is Moses.

When you show your scars and bare your still-healing bruises, you pull back the veil and Jesus is found there. You can live and choose not to tell your story just like you can go see a movie and walk out of the theater never speaking a word of what you were moved by or learned, thought or witnessed. But there is a beauty and a joy unlike anything else that comes with the telling. It may come at a price and your voice might shake, but He has given you something worth sharing, no matter where you find yourself on the pages of your story.

You aren't called to be Moses.

Our stories are not in a competition but if they were, simply live and tell and you win it all.

There's this game I like to play and it never fails to catch people by surprise. Here's how it works: I invite someone to grab coffee and once we've found a comfortable seat and our hands are wrapped around a cup of something delicious, I look into their eyes and say these words: "So, what's your story?"

Try it, I dare you. It's worth it just for the moment of sheer panic that will flash across their face before they hesitantly respond, "My story? What do you mean, exactly?" I then offer to go first, to share with them the pages He has given me to live, and for the record, I don't sugarcoat a single thing. By the time I finish, I can see the relief that has replaced the moment of panic, not because I have masterfully woven together life experiences into a beautiful story but because I have been honest, I have shown the mess of it all, and I've dared to say that the scars that remain are signs of His grace. My tests have truly become my testimony, my mess turning into my message.

After I finish the telling, I turn it over and ask again, "Will you tell me your story?" And this time, instead of panic there is peace. You become a safe place when you share your story, both the broken and the beautiful, with another. And so they begin and every time I am in awe of the broken off pieces and the jagged scars from the hurting places, not because they're messy but because His grace is enough for us all, running in and washing over, healing and mending, changing us and cleansing deep.

I used to hide my scars, the one on my head from brain surgery and the ones on my heart from the times community walked right out. But the scars are still there and they tell the story He gave me to share. I could keep on hiding them but He is teaching me that yes, we've all got a few scars. We've all walked roads that have battered and bruised us, wounding us deep. But the scars tell the stories of battles fought and won, of fears conquered and dreams chased, of mighty healing and of Jesus meeting us in the dry valleys. Your scars tell your story and although you are more than your past, more than what you have experienced, gone through or done, every moment has been used to shape you into a new creation, redeemed and made whole, holy and blameless in the eyes of He who sees your scars and your burnt places, your struggles to join Him and walk on the water, as a page in a best-seller He is joyfully writing.

I think too often we compare our beginning to someone else's middle, our behind-the-scenes to someone else's highlight reel. It's easy to get caught up in comparing our painful places to someone else's promised land, forgetting that we're still journeying and we can trust the unknown of the future to the God we know is authoring its pages. Every sentence He writes is written with the purpose of pointing people to the Friend who is always walking with us. 2 Corinthians says it this way:

Because of this decision we don't evaluate people by what they have or how they look. We looked at the Messiah that way once and got it all wrong, as you know. We certainly don't look at him that way anymore. Now we look inside, and what we see is that anyone united with the Messiah gets a fresh start, is created new. The old life is gone; a new life burgeons!...God has given us the task of telling everyone what he is doing. We're Christ's representatives. God uses us to persuade men and women to drop their differences and enter into God's work of making things right between them. We're speaking for Christ himself now: Become friends with God; he's already a friend with you.[4]

We have been given the task of telling everyone what God is up to in our lives. He has given us a story to live and it may have twists and turns, roads we would rather not walk and ampersands we would prefer to hurry through to the other side, but He calls us to speak from those places and glorify Him on every page, daring to say He is beautiful and true, loving and kind, no matter what story the next page may tell.

Sometimes we can't fully comprehend a moment until time has had its way.

It was the summer of 2013, smack in the middle of falling in love with the power of story, and there I was, a nervous wreck sitting cross-legged on a blown-up and slowly deflating mattress somewhere in the hills of North Carolina.

Through a series of random happenings, my words were scheduled to go live on a website that would reach tens of thousands. I escaped to the back bedroom, opened up my laptop, and scanned the page for my words splashed across the screen. I was both elated and sick to my stomach, tempted to pull it down before anyone could see but also full of hope with the idea that His words through me might reach and encourage even just one person.

I had no idea that the same words that would reach around the world would cause my own world to seemingly implode. Listen, it's a lot easier to write honestly and openly of your scars and your messy places when the only ones who will read are strangers. It's a whole different ballgame when the ones who have seen you walk through those valleys are introduced to your story written out in words and not just life moments. At the time, I wrote for myself and for Him but I didn't share His words through me with anyone I knew in real life. I had been blogging for several years but the word *writer* was something I never once attached to my being.

But sometimes God gives you a preview, a before-taste, and we gobble it up just like we eat all the popcorn before the theater lights dim and the movie begins. We have no idea what will happen before the credits roll although we know the movie will unfold one plot-line at a time, one character twist and curveball moment after another.

I could hear the clock ticking, feel my fingers twitching and the tears falling as my eyes fell on an email that shared a link to the words I hoped no one I knew would ever find. I trusted God with my story and yet I didn't want anyone to really know it, to see the vulnerable places and be able to speak into those, because what if they called everything a mess, what if my story held no significance and had no value?

As I fell asleep I prayed into the dark of night, begging Him to write something beautiful with my story and to use it for His glory, because I sure didn't want to tell of the broken places, of the questions and the loneliness and the darkness, if He wasn't going to be the Hero of it all and if He wasn't going to use it for good somehow, someway.

I woke up to the clock still ticking but my phone was buzzing and the words kept coming and for the very first time in my life, I realized that God had a message and He was using me to tell it.

The Bible promises that we overcome by the word of our testimonies and so it stands to reckon that we have to actually share our stories.[5]

Somehow I had missed the fact that you can type into a computer screen and reach hundreds, maybe thousands, but there are people we pass every day that need to know the Hope that keeps us grounded, the anchor for our souls. They need to hear how we are complete in Christ and that even in the chaos and the unknowns He is faithful.

You have to share when you're scared so they can see that He is Sovereign.

You've got to be vulnerable and open so they can know He is the One signing His name to the story.

You have be honest about the mess so they can see His message weaving all the way through.

The popcorn will run out and the credits will play, but I pray my voice will be telling the story up until the very end.

I had been blogging almost four years before I claimed the word *writer*. I was terrified to attach it to my being because somewhere inside I believed "I know writers and I am not one."

I believed my story was important but at the end of the day, I held up the stick and decided I didn't measure up, couldn't fit the bill or fit the mold or fit in or fit whatever it even takes to be a writer. But He had other plans and He used a blog post and a free-fall to show me that by refusing to claim *writer*, I had been making it about me when it was really only about Him. He fashioned me to write and to use this gift to glorify Him. By refusing to tell my story, I thought I was keeping my heart safe but really I was only denying Him the glory.

Maybe He has fashioned you to be something and it's time you wear what He's given. Maybe it's time you claim what He has given you and live in the power of His goodness, in the light of His love, convinced that He has you right where you are for such a time as now. Maybe it's time we lay down our rocks and build altars, see ourselves as small in light of His beautiful brilliance, and dare to believe He is here with us in the in between.

Maybe, just maybe, the story we're so afraid of sharing is the very story He is going to use to show us once and for all that He has always been there, has always loved us deep and true, has always had a purpose for the pain and we have no reason to reach for the pen in His hands.

Wherever you find yourself reading these words, this is what you've got to know: It isn't always pretty and it's bound to get messy again down the road but in the middle of your mess He is writing your message. Have faith, hold onto hope, and let Love be your guide.

Don't wait for the credits to play. Claim what He has given you and then use it for His glory. Live and tell the story He is writing with your days.

You aren't called to be Moses, but you aren't supposed to be Abraham either.

As I read the words in Romans 4, I find myself drawing my breath in, sudden and quick. Abraham lived many in between days waiting for a child and trusting God's promise, but then Scripture appears to pull back the veil and share one more piece of the puzzle:

If Abraham, by what he did for God, got God to approve of him, he could certainly have taken credit for it. But the story we're given is a God-story, not an Abraham-story. What we read in Scripture is, "Abraham entered into what God was doing for him, and that was the turning point. He trusted God to set him right instead of trying to be right on his own."[6]

The passage goes on to say the promise was not given because of something Abraham might or might not do, but because God decided to bless him and Abraham took Him at His word. "The fulfillment of God's promise depends entirely on trusting God and his way, and then simply embracing him and what he does...Abraham was first named "father" and then became a father because he dared to trust God to do what only God could do: raise the dead to life, with a word make something out of nothing. When everything was hopeless, Abraham believed anyway, deciding to live not on the basis of what he saw he couldn't do but on what God said he would do."[7]

Abraham's story is his because he dared to believe that his story was being written by One who would keep His promise. He trusted that the Author already knew the ending and so he lived in faith, trusting that God would do what He said He would do.

Whatever ampersand you're in, God's got it. You don't have to save the day, you aren't responsible for the healing, and the world is not on your shoulders. It's in His hands and He is a faithful God, ready and able and willing to give you a God-story.

Lord, help us to recognize that our story finds its meaning only in You. Show us that knowing the ending isn't necessary for the here-and-now to be beautiful. Remind us that You turn messes into messages and tests into testimonies.

As we take small steps of bravery, would You surround us with our safe people, the ones who will encourage us, strengthen us, point us to Your Word, and carry our stories gently. We ask also that You take us beyond our safe circle and straight to the ones who need to be encouraged, strengthened, and reassured that their stories matter.

We choose to believe there is power in our stories because You hold the pen. Jesus, we ask that You fill us with Your words before we press publish or walk away from a conversation.

Lord, help us speak our questions in Your presence. Would You remind us over and over that we already have the only answer we will ever need: You. Even as we pray for healing and believe that You can mend what is broken, show us that we have been seen and known and fully loved by You for all of our days. When we are lonely in the middle of it all, when the dark seems to have swallowed us whole and we're desperately searching for the light, meet us there. Remind us that You have been there for every page and every situation and never once, not even for a moment, have we walked alone.

Thank You for the chapters in between — they make us who we are and they show the world how faithful You are. May we live a story that lays stones down in remembrance, a testimony that You have done a good, good work — not because You had to, but because You chose to.

Remind us we are Yours and may we live today in grateful praise, ecstatic with the sheer thought of being a child of the King. We love You and thank You for writing the pages and authoring the story of our lives. You do not make mistakes, nothing that we have walked through was wasted, and You have a purpose for every single moment. May we never try to snatch the pen away.

No matter what tomorrow brings, we will trust You in the ampersand because at the end of the day, even in the questions and even as we pray for healing and hope for life in the dry places, even when we're lonely in the middle of the plot line and even if we aren't sure that we'll see our dreams realized, we know that You are still good, You are still God, and You love us fiercely, madly, deeply. You hold the pen, our lives are the stories, and in the middle of all this mess we still choose to believe You are writing a masterpiece. Even if not, Lord, even if not...

a gift for you

Each image in this book is available as a free full-color download. Visit KaitlynBouchillon.com to sign up for an email subscription and receive all nine prints.

many thanks to these

To my favorite companion, Jesus // These are Your words, not mine. Thank You for trusting me with them, for writing the story I get to live and for walking with me through every page. You are my favorite everything. Every bit of this is for You.

Mom & Dad // Thank you for the many times you've said yes, the times you've said no, the sacrifices made — both those the boys and I are aware of and those we'll never know — and for the gift of growing up in a house that talked about Jesus. I'll put it in print: you have parented well.

The boys // You are the best guys I know. You have seen me at my very worst and you still love me, even with an accent. I wouldn't trade y'all for anything.

Alex, Kendall & Taylor // You have taught me community. God used you three to rewrite my story, to speak truth over the lies, and to point me always back to Him. You have held my hand in the dark times and laughed with me in the best. You are my people and my heart is home when I'm with you. Thank you for giving me a glimpse of what Jesus looks like.

Emerald // You know how deep I believe it, how God would have been good even if not. And you know the miracle of what it looks like when the story continues. Thank you for holding the door wide open for me to share our story. I love doing life together.

My Haiti family // You are all so much more than "just a missions team" to me. Thank you for giving me room to process, encouraging me to share, and for understanding what we've seen and refusing to be silent about it all.

Palmer, Mackenzie, Mary Helen & McKinley // You made my last one the best one. I love you four more than you'll ever know.

Holley // Thank you for listening the very first time I dared to talk about my love for story, for the kind words on the cover of this book, and for one hundred things in between.

My online people // There are people who say online friendships aren't the real deal, but I beg to differ. This book never would have happened without your love and encouragement. I'm eternally grateful for the friendships that have formed through comment threads and computer screens, Voxer messages and handwritten letters.

Jenn, Abby, Tori, Sarah, Lilah & Mary Grace // Your art is beautiful. Thank you for gracing the pages of this book with your gifts.

notes

introduction
1. Daniel 3:16-18, The Voice, emphasis mine.
2. Daniel 3:16-18, MSG, emphasis mine.
3. Daniel 3:26, MSG.
4. Daniel 3:29, MSG.

one // questions & answers
1. Matthew 27:51.
2. John 8:12.
3. Genesis 50:20.

two // sickness & healing
1. Kaitlyn Bouchillon, "I Have a Tumor," *Kaitlyn Bouchillon*, June 30, 2010, http://kaitlynbouchillon.com/2010/06/i-have-a-tumor/.

three // broken & mended
1. Ezekiel 37:5-6.

four // loneliness & community
1. Melanie Shankle, *Nobody's Cuter Than You* (Carol Stream, IL: Tyndale House Publishers Inc., 2015), 77.

five // small & seen
1. This saying is attributed to many, but is often said to be inspired by 2 Corinthians 3:18.

2. Ann Voskamp, *The Greatest Gift* (Carol Stream: Tyndale House Publishers, 2013), 70.
3. Colossians 1:27.
4. Emily Freeman, *Simply Tuesday* (Grand Rapids: Revell, 2015), 20.
5. Jen Hatmaker, *For The Love* (Nashville: Thomas Nelson, 2015), 33.
6. Lara Casey, *Make it Happen* (Nashville: Thomas Nelson, 2014), 182.

six // here and there

1. Tomlin, Chris. *Lord, I Need You.* Passion. 2011. CD.
2. Walker-Smith, Kim. *Holy Spirit (Live).* Jesus Culture. Jeremy Edwardson, 2012. CD.

seven // darkness and light

1. Matthew 4:1-11.
2. Barbara Brown Taylor, *Learning to Walk in the Dark* (New York: HarperOne, 2014), 15.

eight // names & dreams

1. John 14:6.

nine // live & tell

1. C.S. Lewis, *God in the Dock* (Grand Rapids: Eerdmans Publishing Co, 1994), 29.
2. Ian Morgan Cron, *Chasing Francis: A Pilgrim's Tale* (Colorado Springs: NavPress, 2006), 67.
3. Ibid.
4. 2 Corinthians 5:16-17, 20, MSG.
5. Revelation 12:11.
6. Romans 4:1-3, MSG.
7. Romans 4:16-18, MSG.

let's be friends

Dear you,
   It is my hope and prayer that the words in this book have met you right where you are. I truly wish we could meet up for coffee and a delicious brownie to chat about life and all the in betweens. For now, though, we'll have to rely on this fancy thing called the Internet. If you're looking for encouragement or assurance that your story matters – no matter what page you find yourself on – you can find me embracing the mess and living the story at KaitlynBouchillon.com

I would love to see you there! Truly.
kait

(...and all the social things....)

Twitter: @kaitlyn_bouch
Instagram: @kaitlyn_bouch
Facebook: facebook.com/kaitlynebouchillon
Pinterest: pinterest.com/kaitlynbouch

Made in the USA
Las Vegas, NV
22 February 2021

18383584R00108